LONGMAN LITERATURE

The Royal Hunt
of the Sun

Peter Shaffer

Editor: Suzy Graham-Adriani
Glossary prepared by Geoff Barton

Longman 🚢

viviana.

Longman Literature Shakespeare

Series editor: Roy Blatchford
Consultant: Jackie Head

Macbeth   0 582 08827 5 (paper)
            0 582 24592 3 (cased)
Romeo and Juliet   0 582 08836 4 (paper)
            0 582 24591 5 (cased)
The Merchant of Venice   0 582 08835 6 (paper)
            0 582 24593 1 (cased)
A Midsummer Night's Dream   0 582 08833 X (paper)
            0 582 24590 7 (cased)
Julius Caesar   0 582 08828 3 (paper)
            0 582 24589 3 (cased)
Twelfth Night   0 582 08834 8 (paper)
Othello   0 582 09719 3 (paper)
King Lear   0 582 09718 5 (paper)
Hamlet   0 582 09720 7 (paper)
Henry V   0 582 22584 1 (paper)
The Tempest   0 582 22583 3 (paper)
Henry IV Part 1   0 582 23660 6 (paper)
As You Like It   0 582 23661 4 (paper)
Richard III   0 582 23663 0 (paper)

Longman Literature

Series editor: Roy Blatchford

Plays

Alan Ayckbourn   *Absurd Person Singular*   0 582 06020 6
Arthur Miller   *An Enemy of the People*   0 582 09717 7
J B Priestley   *An Inspector Calls*   0 582 06012 5
Terence Rattigan   *The Winslow Boy*   0 582 06019 2
Willy Russell   *Educating Rita*   0 582 06013 3
                Shirley Valentine   0 582 08173 4
Peter Shaffer   *The Royal Hunt of the Sun*   0 582 06014 1
                Equus   0 582 09712 6
Bernard Shaw   *Arms and the Man*   0 582 07785 0
                Pygmalion   0 582 06015 X
                Saint Joan   0 582 07786 9
Oscar Wilde   *The Importance of Being Earnest*   0 582 07784 2

Other titles in the Longman Literatures series are listed on page 110.

▩ Contents

The writer on writing

by Peter Shaffer

An introduction to three plays: *The Royal Hunt of the Sun, Equus* and *Amadeus*

It is hard for me to comment on these plays. I do not much like the idea of an author, as it were, walking along beside his texts pointing out features of interest in them. As a matter of fact, I do not much like anybody else doing so: as I grow older I confess that I have less and less use for criticism, exegesis, or scholarly essays of explication. In America, where I have spent a fair portion of my time, writing seems to have fallen almost entirely into the hands of commentators.

The pages of this volume contain the material of live theatre. They are of no use to the radio director, the television director, even the cinema director. The material is intended to be brought to physical life in a space which has to be animated afresh each time of playing by the vibrations of the actors and by those of the spectators. A play, like justice, is pre-eminently a thing *seen* to be done.

This is why, I hope, these three plays possess certain features in common. Each owns a certain flamboyance: a reliance upon gesture to enshrine idea – without which there is no theatre; a desire to enthral a crowd of watchers – without which there is certainly no theatre; and a strong pleasure in illusion. I imagine that this pleasure has always been a motive with me, ever since as a young boy I laid out a pack of cards on my pillow in bed, and imagined the lives of the Kings, Queens and Jacks rather than play games with them.

It is my object to tell tales; to conjure the spectres of horror and happiness, and fill other heads with the images which have haunted my own. My desire, I suppose, is to perturb and make gasp: to please and make laugh: to surprise. If I am a peacock in this respect, at least I am aware that peacockery is one of the dramatist's obligations. 'Don't show off' is not an adjuration to be made sensibly to playwrights. Needless to say, this does not exonerate in me, or in any writer, excessive spreading of tail-feathers.

The Royal Hunt of the Sun, the earliest of the three, was produced most splendidly by John Dexter and the National Theatre at the Chichester Festival of 1964. Speaking of tail-feathers, I think that this celebrated production used up the entire (and considerable) stock of Chinese pheasant feathers available in England at that time. It was a hugely lavish affair, superbly set and costumed by Michael Annals. The colour supplements of two Sunday newspapers in London devoted astonished articles to its lavishness: this sort of spectacle had not been seen on drab English stages for some while. Audiences responded in tremendous and delighted numbers. To this day I still receive communications from people telling me how they can never forget the opening of the great metal sun near the beginning of the play, or the flood of blood red cloth vomiting out of it later to engulf them in the idea of massacre, or the golden funeral masks of the Incas, with their triangular eyes and copper cheeks, turned yearningly towards the rising sun at the end. This was not lavishness for the sake of it: lavishness was the point. Peru was a kingdom, wrote one mediaeval commentator, where gold was as common as wood in Spain. There was clearly no showing a kingdom of infinite treasures without recourse to some visual splendour. Similarly there was no creating the aural world of sixteenth-century Peru without a strange and continuing music. Many of my plays have used music, but none more elaborately than *The Royal Hunt of the Sun*. In my view, Marc Wilkinson's superb score is integral to the play.

Of course I do not mean to imply by any of the above that the words are not important. They are paramount. *The Royal Hunt of the Sun* took me three years to write. So did *Equus*. So did *Amadeus*. I write and destroy the writing; and rewrite, and destroy the rewriting – and I continue in this way until not only the images but the words are entirely clear in my mind, and the flavour of each scene is strong on my tongue. Each play has obviously to acquire a different kind of flavour – the three under discussion here are, after all, set in mediaeval Peru, modern Hampshire, and Enlightenment Vienna respectively; but all are obviously contemporary pieces in the sense that they were written by me and are being read by you.

Equus is obviously less rhetorical than *The Royal Hunt of the Sun*, but many of the same elements appear in it. Again there are masks, only they are now transparent: we see the actor's head through the wire head of the horse – a double image which is the preoccupation of the play. Once again there are raised boots, as in ancient theatre: the Inca in *Royal Hunt* appears before the massacre poised on huge cothurni; the horses stalk and stamp round their English stable on high metal hooves. The sound of their feet on the wooden stage, discreetly and alarmingly used, filled the theatre when the play was first produced at the National Theatre in 1973 (again by John Dexter) with an ominous scraping which seemed to herald divine presence. Once more there was music by Marc Wilkinson, this time an eerie humming in twelve tones to recall – in the composer's intention – Vienna, the city of Freud. Perhaps this last was a tenuous connection. All the same the play, as it grew under my hands, came more and more to question the ultimate uses of psychiatry. In the first draft the doctor was drawn more vaguely; less in the central position. In the second draft he grew more prominent, and his self-doubts more important to the meaning of the piece. In London *Equus* caused a sensation because it displayed cruelty to horses; in New York because it allegedly displayed cruelty to psychiatrists.

Of all my plays *Equus* was the most private. I wrote it for myself. I had no notion how popular it was to become – its extraordinary run of well over a thousand performances on Broadway could never have been remotely envisaged by me. The play has been subject to a vast amount of commentary and misuse: a few doctors declaring it a madman's charter; some do-your-own thingers using it as a means to justify every kind of human aberration. For me it is a deeply erotic play, and also one of tragic conflict. Tragedy obviously does not lie in a conflict of Right and Wrong, but in a collision between two different kinds of Right: in this case, surely, between Dysart's professional obligation to treat a terrified boy who has committed a dreadful crime, and Alan's passionate capacity for worship – his profound desire to cry *O Magnum Mysterium!* alone in a rubbish-strewn field, his burning ecstasy set against his doctor's careful prosaicism. Dysart has to do what he does. Let no man say *Do your own thing*, for example, to Jack the Ripper. Yet in proceeding by his best and honourable lights, the doctor cannot but know that he is in some clear sense the destroyer of a passion he must forever, and rightly, envy.

Envy, of course, is also the theme of **Amadeus**: Salieri's envy of Mozart's genius. Again I have little to add about this play: what I needed to say on the theme of man's proper objection to divine arbitrariness seems to me to be fairly contained in the work itself. Of course Salieri commits a stupid sin — and I do not mean his persecution of Mozart. He demands a God he can understand. What artist would do that? He says, in effect, *Let me dip my net into the unfathomable well, and bring up shining creatures hitherto unseen!* But he also says, *Let me see to the bottom of this well: it is my right as a man! I object to the darkness wherein the connections of beauty are formed.* As well object to the dark of the womb! Confronted by divine mystery, he says merely, *How dare you?* A fool, you say. And yet he also has his right. (Again the collision of *Rights*.) All he wanted was to serve. To be owned by an Absolute. We need an answer for his torment. True he is condemned to chew forever the cud of his own poisonous sense of fairness — but yet who would dare say that a sense of fairness is dispensable?

Paul Scofield played Salieri at the National Theatre in November 1979, and in New York Ian McKellen played the same part a year later, somewhat rewritten. The reasons for the changes, which were approved by audiences and critics who saw both versions, are explained in my preface to the new edition of the play.

In the end, I suppose, all three pieces share a common preoccupation with worship and man's attempts to acquire or murder a special divinity. This must indicate, surely, my own belief in its utter indispensability to our lives.

Introduction

The Royal Hunt of the Sun was first staged at the Chichester festival in July 1964. For Peter Shaffer it represented a departure – moving from detective stories, naturalistic plays and farce to epic theatre and the use of new ('avant-garde') methods of staging. The play was an instant success.

The play's impact on its first audiences can be better understood if we consider that British acting in 1964 was, in general, largely concerned with actors being good at the spoken delivery of lines and being able to convey subtle shades of meaning in individual words. Theatre action, as a whole, was largely naturalistic rather than athletic or physical.

Two productions from that year – *The Royal Hunt of the Sun* and Peter Brook's *The Marat/Sade* – helped to change this reputation, and inspired many future British productions to explore the visual dimension of the stage.

You will see that the play is in two acts, each in twelve sections. It focuses on the conquest of Peru by Francisco Pizarro: the historical phenomenon in which 167 Spanish conquistadors subdued an empire of 24 million. These events were described in W H Prescott's *The Conquest of Peru* (written in the nineteenth century) and greatly impressed Shaffer. In the story of the clash between Catholic and Inca beliefs and ways of life, Shaffer saw a parallel with modern confrontations over different forms of government – for example, the clash between imperialism (empire building) and communism. In his play, though, he examines this conflict through individuals, using Pizarro and Atahuallpa, the Inca King, as opposites, both in physical terms and in terms of the cultures and political systems that they represent.

The story is told through Old Martin, a passionate narrator who has had an integral role in the action. A series of vivid flashbacks focuses the audience's attention on an exploration of two important philosophical issues – the loss of faith and the search for meaning in life.

The Incas have peace, stability and gold. The Spaniards, under the leadership of the atheist Pizarro, have courage, avarice and guns – and Christ. In His name they set about stripping the empire of its gold, social order and freedom, as well as destroying individual lives. It is Pizarro's quest that is reflected in the play's title. He is a rugged man who, in the first instance, seems to be in search of gold. However, his quest develops into something more significant. Confronted by the Sun King Atahuallpa's unearthly qualities and blind faith in his own immortality, Pizarro begins to hope that he himself can once again believe that a man can die and on the third day rise again. To discover this, it is necessary for him to become a hunter. Atahuallpa becomes the exotic bird that Pizarro must *blow out of the sky*. Strong visual images of him hovering high up in his father Sun develop into his becoming *the robber bird* who is caught by the hunter. Though Pizarro rejects notions of honour, his instincts nonetheless make him recoil from killing his captured enemy. Ultimately it is his enemy's unsinkable, almost seraphic confidence in his own ability to rise again from the dead that gradually moves Pizarro into action. He is suddenly filled with hope: if Atahuallpa can rise from the grave, then why not Christ?

As well as offering an insight into the mysterious Inca world, *The Royal Hunt of the Sun* also offers opportunities for exotic spectacle. Undoubtedly it should be breathtaking to look at. It calls for a comparatively simple set, but a constant variety of effects. The first presentation brought a spectacular dimension to the National Theatre's work. In fact, some critics complained that it was *too* spectacular, *too* lavish at the expense of dialogue and character.

The challenges the play offers are colossal. John Dexter – who first directed it – admitted that he was first attracted to it by the casual stage direction which caught his eye when thumbing through the script – *they cross the Andes*. His imagination started to picture how this could be achieved by mime alone, for obviously the Andes could not be built on stage! A further challenge was the need to create an appropriate atmosphere that would generate excitement in the theatre. His solution was to present the episode through bold physical action.

The 1964 audience's introduction to the Inca world was a memorable moment, as one of the reviewers of the original production recalled:

> *The stage bursts into glorious life when the Spaniards finally reach the Inca capital and a huge golden motif backstage suddenly opens out, petal by petal, like a great sunflower, to reveal the immobile form of Atahuallpa, the Inca Sun-King, a scintillating figure in white and gold.*

In addition to such vivid spectacle, sound is also an essential ingredient in building atmosphere and dramatic tension, and one that Shaffer incorporates in many of his plays. Pulsating drum beats, strange plaintive music from reed pipes, cymbals and giant maracas, bird cries, plain chant and organ music formed some of the original score. Terrifying sounds accompanied the action as Indians scattered in hysterical confusion, cut down by the Spanish troops. And the great massacre was further symbolised by a gigantic bloodstained cloth which billowed out over the stage. Shaffer wrote of Marc Wilkinson's music:

> To me its most memorable items are the exquisitely doleful lament which opens Act 2, and most amazingly of all, the final chant of Resurrection, to be whined and whispered, howled and hooted, over Atahuallpa's body in the darkness, before the last sunrise of the Inca Empire.

Undoubtedly *The Royal Hunt of the Sun* would be a costly and ambitious play to produce on a grand scale, since it requires a large cast, and from the script descriptions, many changes of set. It is worth bearing in mind, however, that its demands on the imagination need not always be a demand on the budget. Michael Annals, the original set designer, constructed the brilliant glowing sun from beaten-out bottle tops!

We have here an adventure story. But it is an adventure story that also plunges the spectator into a thought-provoking network of powerful themes and ideas. We see, for example, the corrupting influence of commercial Christianity. And we see so-called civilised men who are still unable to resist cult, ritual and the power of deities, even when those deities are false.

The audience's sympathy lies largely with Atahuallpa, victim of the Spanish invasion and Pizarro's broken word. He alone retains his nobility to the end. But what is really absorbing in the play is the relationship between the two leaders. Both are rivals in terms of survival and history; yet each comes hauntingly closer to understanding the spirit of the other. In this way, the play highlights Shaffer's fascination with the endless ambiguity of the human situation, of the conflict between two different kinds of 'right'. (See 'The writer on writing', page vi.)

Reading log

One of the easiest ways of keeping track of your reading is to keep a log book. This can be any exercise book or folder that you have to hand, but make sure you reserve it exclusively for reflecting on your reading, both at home and in school.

As you read the play, stop from time to time and think back over what you have read.

- Is there anything that puzzles you? Note down some questions that you might want to research, discuss with your friends, or ask a teacher. Also note any quotations which strike you as important or memorable.

- Does your reading remind you of anything else you have read, heard or seen on TV or at the cinema? Jot down what it is and where the similarities lie.

- Have you had any experiences similar to those narrated in the play? Do you find yourself identifying closely with one or more of the characters? Record this as accurately as you can.

- Do you find yourself really liking, or really loathing, any of the characters? What is it about them that makes you feel so strongly? Make notes that you can add to.

- Can you picture the locations and settings? Draw maps, plans, diagrams, drawings, in fact any doodle that helps you make sense of these things.

- Now and again try to predict what will happen next in the play. Use what you already know of the author, the genre (type of story) and the characters to help you do this. Later record how close you were and whether you are surprised at the outcome.

- Write down any feelings that you have about the play. Your reading log should help you make sense of your own ideas alongside those of the author.

AUTHOR'S NOTES

THE TEXT

Each Act contains twelve sections, marked by roman numerals. These are solely for reference, and do not indicate pauses or breaks of any kind. The action is continuous.

THE SET

In this version of the play I refer throughout to the set used by the National Theatre Company at the Chichester Festival 1964. Essentially, all that is required for a production of *The Royal Hunt of the Sun* is a bare stage and an upper level. However, the setting by Michael Annals was so superb, and so brilliantly succeeded in solving the visual problems of the play, that I wish to recall it here in print.

Basically this design consisted of a huge aluminium ring, twelve feet in diameter, hung in the centre of a plain wooden back-wall. Around its circumference were hinged twelve petals. When closed, these interlocked to form a great medallion on which was incised the emblem of the Conquistadors; when opened, they formed the rays of a giant golden sun, emblem of the Incas. Each petal had an inlay of gold magnetized to it: when these inlays were pulled out (in Act II, Scene vi) the great black frame remaining symbolized magnificently the desecration of Peru. The centre of this sun formed an acting area above the stage, which was used in Act I to show Atahuallpa in majesty, and in Act II served for his prison and subsequently for the treasure chamber.

This simple but amazing set was for me totally satisfying on all levels: scenically, aesthetically, and symbolically.

THE MUSIC

The musical excerpts at the end of the book represent the three most easily detached pieces from the remarkable score

B

composed for the play by Marc Wilkinson. This extraordinary music I believe to be an integral part of any production of *The Royal Hunt of the Sun*. It embraces bird cries; plain-chant; a fantasia for organ; freezing sounds for the Mime of the Great Ascent, and frightening ones for the Mime of the Great Massacre. To me its most memorable items are the exquisitely doleful lament which opens Act II, and, most amazing of all, the final Chant of Resurrection, to be whined and whispered, howled and hooted, over Atahuallpa's body in the darkness, before the last sunrise of the Inca Empire.

The full score can be obtained from London Management, 235 Regent Street, London W.1.

THE PRODUCTION

There are, no doubt, many ways of producing this play, as there are of setting it. My hope was always to realise on stage a kind of 'total' theatre, involving not only words but rites, mimes, masks and magics. The text cries for illustration. It is a director's piece, a pantomimist's piece, a musician's piece, a designer's piece, and of course an actor's piece, almost as much as it is an author's. In this edition, as with the set, I have included as many details of the Chichester production as possible, partly because I was deeply involved in its creation, but mainly as a tribute to the superb achievement of John Dexter.

P.S.

Characters of the Play

THE SPANIARDS

The Officers

FRANCISCO PIZARRO, *Commander of the Expedition*
HERNANDO DE SOTO, *Second-in-Command*
MIGUEL ESTETE, *Royal Veedor, or Overseer*
PEDRO DE CANDIA, *Commander of Artillery*
DIEGO DE TRUJILLO, *Master of Horse*

The Men

MARTIN RUIZ
YOUNG MARTIN, *Pizarro's Page: Old Martin as a boy*
SALINAS, *Blacksmith*
RODAS, *Tailor*
VASCA
DOMINGO
JUAN CHAVEZ
PEDRO CHAVEZ

The Priests

FRAY VINCENTE DE VALVERDE, *Chaplain to the
Expedition (Dominican)*
FRAY MARCOS DE NIZZA, *Franciscan Friar*

THE INDIANS

ATAHUALLPA, *Sovereign Inca of Peru*
VILLAC UMU, *High Priest of Peru*
CHALLCUCHIMA, *An Inca General*
A CHIEFTAIN
A HEADMAN OF A THOUSAND FAMILIES
FELIPILLO, *An Indian boy, employed by Pizarro as
Interpreter*
MANCO, *A Chasqui, or Messenger* (non-speaking)
INTI COUSSI, *Step-sister of Atahuallpa* (non-speaking)
OELLO, *A wife of Atahuallpa* (non-speaking)
SPANISH SOLDIERS AND PERUVIAN INDIANS

Place

Apart from two early scenes in Spain and Panama, the play is set in the Upper Province of the Inca Empire: what is now South Ecuador and North Western Peru. The whole of Act II takes place in the town of Cajamarca.

Time

June 1529 – August 1533

Act I

The Hunt

Act II

The Kill

The Royal Hunt of the Sun

For Alan and Paula
With love

agessiv, violent personality.
not guy - person - or man
             about 18 years old.

He didn't agree

The books end with.

would

Act One

A bare stage. On the back wall, which is of wood, hangs a huge metal medallion, quartered by four black crucifixes, sharpened to resemble swords.

I

Darkness.

OLD MARTIN, *grizzled, in his middle fifties, appears. He wears the black costume of a Spanish hidalgo in the mid-sixteenth century.*

OLD MARTIN. Save you all. My name is Martin. I'm a soldier of Spain and that's it. Most of my life I've spent fighting for land, treasure and the cross. I'm worth millions. Soon I'll be dead and they'll bury me out here in Peru, the land I helped ruin as a boy. This story is about ruin. Ruin and gold. More gold than any of you will ever see even if you worked in a counting house. I'm going to tell you how one hundred and sixty-seven men conquered an empire of twenty-four million. And then things that no one has ever told: things to make you groan and cry out I'm lying. And perhaps I am. The air of Peru is cold and sour like in a vault, and wits turn easier here even than in Europe. But grant me this: I saw him closer than anyone, and had cause only to love him. He was my altar, my bright image of salvation. Francisco Pizarro! Time was when I'd have died for him, or for any worship.

YOUNG MARTIN *enters duelling an invisible opponent with a stick. He is Old Martin as an impetuous boy of fifteen.* If you could only imagine what it was like for me at the beginning, to be allowed to serve him. But boys don't dream like that any more – service! Conquest! Riding down Indians in the name of Spain. The inside of my head was one vast plain for feats of daring. I used to lie up in the hayloft for hours reading my Bible – Don Cristobal on the rules of Chivalry. And then he came and made them real. And the only wish of my life is that I had never seen him.

FRANCISCO PIZARRO *comes in. He is a man in late middle age: tough, commanding, harsh, wasted, secret. The gestures are blunt and often violent; the expression intense and energetic, capable of fury and cruelty, but also of sudden melancholy and sardonic humour. At the moment he appears more neatly than he is ever to do again: hair and beard are trimmed, and his clothes quite grand, as if he is trying to make a fine impression.*

He is accompanied by his Second in Command, HERNANDO DE SOTO, *and the Dominican* FRAY VINCENTE DE VALVERDE. DE SOTO *is an impressive figure in his forties: his whole air breathes an unquestioning loyalty – to his profession, his faith, and to accepted values. He is an admirable soldier and a staunch friend.* VALVERDE *on the other hand is a peasant Priest whose zeal is not greatly tempered by intelligence, nor sweetened by any anxiety to please.*

PIZARRO. I was suckled by a sow. My house is the oldest in Spain – the pig-sty.

OLD MARTIN. He'd made two expeditions to the New World already. Now at over sixty years old he was back in Spain, making one last try. He'd shown the King enough gold to get sole right of discovery in Peru and the title of Viceroy over anything he conquered. In return he was to fit out an army at his own expense. He started recruiting in his own birthplace, Trujillo.

Lights up below as he speaks. Several Spanish villagers have entered, among them SALINAS, *a blacksmith,* RODAS, *a tailor,* VASCA, DOMINGO *and the* CHAVEZ *brothers.* PIZARRO *addresses* DIEGO, *a young man of twenty-five.*

PIZARRO. What's your name?

DIEGO. Diego, sir.

PIZARRO. What do you know best?

DIEGO. Horses I suppose, if I was to name anything.

PIZARRO. How would you feel to be Master of Horse, Diego?

DIEGO (*eagerly*). Sir!

PIZARRO. Go over there. Who's smith here?

SALINAS. I am.

PIZARRO. Are you with us?

SALINAS. I'm not against you.

PIZARRO. Who's your friend?

RODAS. Tailor, if it's your business.

PIZARRO. Soldiers never stop mending and patching. They'll be grateful for your assistance.

RODAS. Well find some other fool to give it to them. I'm resting here.

PIZARRO. Rest. (*To* YOUNG MARTIN) Who's this?

DIEGO. Martin Ruiz, sir. A good lad. He knows all his codes of Chivalry by heart. He's aching to be a page, sir.

PIZARRO. How old?

OLD MARTIN. Seventeen.

PIZARRO. Don't lie.

YOUNG MARTIN. Fifteen, sir.

OLD MARTIN *goes off.*

PIZARRO. Parents?

YOUNG MARTIN. Dead, sir.

PIZARRO. Can you write?

YOUNG MARTIN. Two hundred Latin words. Three hundred Spanish.

PIZARRO. Why do you want to come?

YOUNG MARTIN. It's going to be glorious, sir.

PIZARRO. Look you, if you served me you'd be Page to an old slogger: no titles, no traditions. I learnt my trade as a mercenary, going with who best paid me. It's a closed book to me, all that chivalry. But then, not reading or writing, all books are closed to me. If I took you you'd have to be my reader and writer, both.

YOUNG MARTIN. I'd be honoured my Lord. Oh, please my Lord!

PIZARRO. General will do. Let's see your respect. Greet me.

(*The boy bows.*) Now to the Church. That's Brother Valverde, our Chaplain.

VALVERDE. The blessing of God on you, my son. And on all who come with us to alter the heathen.

PIZARRO. Now to our Second-in-Command, Cavalier de Soto. I'm sure you all know the Cavalier well by reputation: a great soldier. He has fought under Cordoba! No expedition he seconds can fail. (*He takes a roll of cloth, woven with the design of a llama, from* DE SOTO.) Now look at this! Indian stuff! Ten years ago standing with the great Balboa, I saw a chieftain draw this beast on the leaf of an aloe. And he said to me: Where this roams is uncountable wealth!

RODAS. Oh, yes, uncountable! Ask Sanchez the farrier about that. He listened to talk like that from him five years ago.

DIEGO. Who cares about him?

RODAS. Uncountable bloody wealth? It rained six months and his skin rotted on him. They lost twenty-seven out of fifty.

PIZARRO. And so we may again. What do you think I'm offering? A walk in the country? Jellies and wine in a basket, your hand round your girl? No, I'm promising you swamps. A forest like the beard of the world. Sitting half-buried in earth to escape the mouths of insects. You may live for weeks on palm tree buds and soup made out of leather straps. And at night you will sleep in thick wet darkness with snakes hung over your heads like bell ropes – and black men in that blackness: men that eat each other. And why should you endure all this? Because I believe that beyond this terrible place is a kingdom, where gold is as common as wood is here! I took only two steps in and found cups and pans made out of it solid.

He claps his hands. FELIPILLO *comes in. He is a slim, delicate Indian from Ecuador, loaded with golden ornaments. In actuality* FELIPILLO *is a treacherous and hysterical creature, but at the moment, under his master's eye, he sways forward before the stupefied villagers with a demure grace.*

4

I present Felipillo, captured on my last trip. Look close at his ornaments. To him they are no more than feathers are to us, but they are all gold, my friends. Examine him. Down!

The villagers examine him.

VALVERDE. Look at him well. This is a heathen. A being condemned to eternal flame unless you help him. Don't think we are merely going to destroy his people and lift their wealth. We are going to take from them what they don't value, and give them instead the priceless mercy of heaven. He who helps me lift this dark man into light I absolve of all crimes he ever committed.

PIZARRO. Well?

SALINAS. That's gold right enough.

PIZARRO. And for your taking. I was like you once. Sitting the afternoon away in this same street, drunk in the inn, to bed in the sty. Stink and mud and nothing to look for. Even if you die with me, what's so tender precious to hold you here?

VASCA. You're pissing right!

PIZARRO. I tell you, man: over there you'll be the masters – that'll be your slave.

VASCA. Well, there's a thought: talk about the slave of slaves!

DOMINGO (*timidly*). Do you think it's true?

PIZARRO. Do you say I lie?

DOMINGO. Oh, no, sir . . .

VASCA. Even if he does, what's to keep you here? You're a cooper: how many casks have you made this year? That's no employment for a dog.

PIZARRO. How about you? You're brothers aren't you?

DIEGO. That's the Chavez brothers, Juan and Pedro.

JUAN. Sir.

PEDRO. Sir.

PIZARRO. Well, what d'you say?

JUAN. I say right, sir.

PEDRO. Me too.

VASCA. And me. I'm going to get a slave or two like him.

DOMINGO. And me. Vasca's right, you can't do worse than stay here.

RODAS. Well not me, boys. Just you catch Rodas marching through any pissing jungle!

SALINAS. Oh, shut your ape's face. Are you going to sit here for ever and pick fleas? He'll come sir.

PIZARRO. Make your way to Toledo for the muster. Diego, enrol them all and take them along.

DIEGO. Sir!

> YOUNG MARTIN *makes to go off with the rest.*
>
> PIZARRO *stays him.*

PIZARRO. Boy.

YOUNG MARTIN. Sir.

> *A pause.*

PIZARRO. Master me the names of all officers and men so far listed.

YOUNG MARTIN. Oh, sir! Yes, sir! Thank you, sir!

PIZARRO. You're a page now, so act like one. Dignity at all times.

YOUNG MARTIN (*bowing*). Yes, sir.

PIZARRO. Respect.

YOUNG MARTIN (*bowing*). Yes, sir.

PIZARRO. And obedience.

YOUNG MARTIN (*bowing*). Yes, sir.

PIZARRO. And it isn't necessary to salute every ten seconds.

YOUNG MARTIN (*bowing*). No, sir.

VALVERDE. Come, my son, there's work to do.

> *They go off.*

PIZARRO. Strange sight, yourself, just as you were in this very street.

DE SOTO. Do you like it?

PIZARRO. No, I was a fool. Dreamers deserve what they get.

DE SOTO. And what are you dreaming about now?

PIZARRO. Gold.

DE SOTO. Oh, come. Gold is not enough lodestone for you, not any more to drag you back to the new world.

PIZARRO. You're right. At my age things become what they really are. Gold turns into metal.

DE SOTO. Then why? You could stay here now and be hero for a province. What's left to endure so much for – especially with your infirmity? You've earned the right to comfort. Your country would gladly grant it to you for the rest of your life.

PIZARRO. My country, where is that?

DE SOTO. Spain, sir.

PIZARRO. Spain and I have been strangers since I was a boy. The only spot I know in it is here – this filthy village. This is Spain to me. Is this where you wish me comfort? For twenty-two years I drove pigs down this street because my father couldn't own to my mother. Twenty-two years without one single day of hope. When I turned soldier and dragged my arquebus along the roads of Italy, I was so famished I was beyond eating. I got nothing and I gave nothing, and though I groaned for that once I'm glad with it now. Because I owe nothing . . . Once the world could have had me for a petty farm, two rocky fields and a Senor to my name. It said 'No'. Ten years on it could have had me for double – small estate, fifty oranges and a Sir to them. It said 'No'. Twenty years more and it could still have had me cheap: Balboa's trusty lieutenant, marched with him into the Pacific and claimed it for Spain: State Pension and dinner once a week with the local Mayor. But the world said 'No'. Said 'No' and said 'No'. Well, now it's going to know me. If I live this next year I'm going to get a name that won't ever be forgotten. A name to be sung here for centuries in your ballads, out there under the cork trees where I sat as a boy with bandages for shoes. I amuse you.

DE SOTO. Surely you see you don't.

PIZARRO. Oh, yes, I amuse you Cavalier de Soto. The old pigherd lumbering after fame. You inherited your honour – I had to root for mine like the pigs. It's amusing.

II

Lights whiter, colder.

He kneels. An organ sounds: the austere polyphony of Spanish celebration. VALVERDE *enters, bearing an immense wooden Christ. He is accompanied by his assistant,* FRAY MARCOS DE NIZZA, *a Franciscan, a man of far more serene temper and intellectual maturity. All the villagers come in also, wearing the white cloaks of chivalry and carrying banners. Among them is* PEDRO DE CANDIA, *a Venetian captain, wearing a pearl in one ear and walking with a lazy stealth that at once suggests danger.* OLD MARTIN *comes in.*

OLD MARTIN. On the day of St John the Evangelist, our weapons were consecrated in the Cathedral Church of Panama. Our muster was one hundred and eighty-seven, with horses for twenty-seven.

VALVERDE. You are the huntsmen of God. The weapons you draw are sacred! Oh, God, invest us all with the courage of Thy unflinching Son. Show us our way to beat the savage out of his dark forests on to the broad plain of Thy Grace.

DE NIZZA. And comfort, we pray, all warriors that shall be in affliction from this setting out.

OLD MARTIN. Fray Marcos de Nizza, Franciscan, appointed to assist Valverde.

DE NIZZA. You are the bringers of food to starving peoples. You go to break mercy with them like bread, and outpour gentleness into their cups. You will lay before them the inexhaustible table of free spirit, and invite to it all who have dieted on terror. You will bring to all tribes the nourishment of pity. You will sow their fields with love, and teach them to harvest the crop of it, each yield in its season. Remember this always: we are their New World.

VALVERDE. Approach all and be blessed.

During this, the men kneel and are blessed.

OLD MARTIN. Pedro de Candia, Cavalier from Venice, in

charge of weapons and artillery. These villagers you know already. There were many others of course. Almagro, the General's partner, who stayed to organize reinforcements and follow in three months. Riquelme the Treasurer. Pedro of Ayala and Blas of Atienza. Herrada the Swordsman and Gonzales of Toledo. And Juan de Barbaran whom everyone called the good servant out of love for him. And many smaller men. Even its youngest member saw himself with a following of Indians and a province for an orchard. It was a tumbled company, none too noble but ginger for wealth.

Enter E S T E T E: *a stiff, haughty man, dressed in the black of the Spanish court.*

And chiefly there was—

E S T E T E. Miguel Estete. Royal Veedor, and Overseer in the name of King Carlos the Fifth. You should not have allowed anyone to be blessed before me.

P I Z A R R O. Your pardon, Veedor, I don't understand affairs of before and after.

E S T E T E. That is evident. General, on this expedition my name is the law: it is spoken with the King's authority.

P I Z A R R O. Your pardon, but on this expedition my name is the law: there will be no other.

E S T E T E. In matters military.

P I Z A R R O. In all matters.

E S T E T E. In all that do not infringe the majesty of the King.

P I Z A R R O. What matters could?

E S T E T E. Remember your duty to God, sir, and to the throne, sir, and you will not discover them.

P I Z A R R O (*furious*). De Soto! In the name of Spain our holy country, I invest you as second in Command to me. Subject only to me. In the name of Spain our Holy country – I – I –. (*He falters, clutching his side in pain. A pause. The men whisper among themselves*) Take the banners out . . .

D E S O T O. Take up your banners. March!

The organ music continues: all march out leaving P I Z A R R O *and his* P A G E *alone on the stage. Only*

when all the rest are gone does the General collapse.
The boy is frightened and concerned.

YOUNG MARTIN. What is it, sir?

PIZARRO. A wound from long ago. A knife to the bone. A savage put it into me for life. It troubles me at times . . . You'll start long before me with your wounds. With your killing too. I wonder how you'll like that.

YOUNG MARTIN. You watch me, sir.

PIZARRO. I will. You deal in deaths when you are a soldier, and all your study should be to make them clean, what scratches kill and how to cut them.

YOUNG MARTIN. But surely, sir, there's more to soldiering than that?

PIZARRO. You mean, honour, glory – traditions of the service?

YOUNG MARTIN. Yes, sir.

PIZARRO. Dungballs. Soldiers are for killing: that's their reason.

YOUNG MARTIN. But, sir –

PIZARRO. What?

YOUNG MARTIN. It's not just killing.

PIZARRO. Look, boy: know something. Men cannot just stand as men in this world. It's too big for them and they grow scared. So they build themselves shelters against the bigness, do you see? They call the shelters Court, Army, Church. They're useful against loneliness, Martin, but they're not true. They're not real, Martin, Do you see?

YOUNG MARTIN. No, sir. Not truthfully sir . . .

PIZARRO. No, sir. Not truthfully sir! Why must you be so young? Look at you. Only a quarter formed. A colt the world will break for its sightless track. Listen once. Army loyalty is blasphemy. The world of soldiers is a yard of ungrowable children. They play with ribbons and make up ceremonies just to keep out the rest of the world. They add up the number of their blue dead and their green dead and call that their history. But all this is just the flower the bandit carves on his knife before shoving it into a man's side . . . What's Army Tradition? Nothing but years of Us against Them. Christ-men against Pagan-men. Men against men. I've had a life of it boy, and let me tell you it's nothing but a nightmare game, played by brutes to give themselves a reason.

YOUNG MARTIN. But sir, a noble reason can make a fight glorious.

PIZARRO. Give me a reason that stays noble once you start hacking off limbs in its name. There isn't a cause in the world to set against this pain. Noble's a word. Leave it for the books.

YOUNG MARTIN. I can't believe that, sir.

PIZARRO. Look at you – hope, lovely hope, it's on you like dew. Do you know where you're going? Into the forest. A hundred miles of dark and screaming. The dark we all came out of, hot. Things flying, fleeing, falling dead – and their death unnoticed. Take your noble reasons there, Martin. Pitch your silk flags in that black and wave your crosses at the wild cats. See what awe they command. Be advised, boy. Go back to Spain.

YOUNG MARTIN. No, sir. I'm coming with you. I can learn, sir.

PIZARRO. You will be taught. Not by me. The forest.

He stumps out.

III

The boy is left alone. The stage darkens and the huge medallion high on the back wall begins to glow. Great cries of 'Inca!' are heard. The boy bolts off stage. Exotic music mixes with the chanting. Slowly the medallion opens outwards to form a huge golden sun with twelve great rays. In the centre stands ATAHUALLPA, *sovereign Inca of Peru, masked, crowned, and dressed in gold. When he speaks, his voice, like the voices of all the Incas, is strangely formalized.*

Enter below the Inca court: VILLAC UMU, *the High Priest,* CHALLCUCHIMA, MANCO *and others, all masked, and robed in terracotta. They prostrate themselves.*

MANCO. Atahuallpa! God!

ATAHUALLPA. God hears.

MANCO. Manco your Chasqui speaks. I bring truth from many runners what has been seen in the Farthest Province. White men sitting on huge sheep. The sheep are red! Everywhere their leader shouts aloud 'Here is God!'

ATAHUALLPA. The White God!

VILLAC UMU. Beware, beware Inca!

ATAHUALLPA. All-powerful spirit who left this place before my ancestors ruled you. The White God returns!

CHALLCUCHIMA. You do not know this.

ATAHUALLPA. He has been long waited for. If he comes, it is with blessing. Then my people will see I did well to take the Crown.

VILLAC UMU. Ware you! Your mother Moon wears a veil of green fire. An eagle fell on to the temple in Cuzco.

MANCO. It is true, Capac. He fell out of the sky.

VILLAC UMU. Out of a green sky.

CHALLCUCHIMA. On to a house of gold.

VILLAC UMU. When the world ends, small birds grow sharp claws.

ATAHUALLPA. Cover your mouth. (*All cover their mouths*). If the White God comes to bless me, all must see him.

> *The Court retires.* ATAHUALLPA *remains on stage, motionless in his sunflower. He stays in this position until the end of Scene VII.*

IV

Mottled light.
Province of Tumbez. Screams and whoops of alarm imitating tropical bird cries. A horde of Indians rushes across the stage pursued by soldiers.

DE CANDIA. Grab that one! That's the chief.

*They capture the Chieftain. At the sight of this, all
the Indians fall silent and passive.* DE CANDIA
approaches him with drawn sword.

Now, you brownie bastard, show us gold.

PIZARRO. Gently, De Candia. You'll get nothing from him
in terror.

DE CANDIA. Let's see.

PIZARRO. God's wounds! Put up! Felipillo, ask for gold.

FELIPILLO *adopts a set of stylized gestures for his
interpreting, in the manner of sign language.*

CHIEF. We have no gold. All was taken by the great King
in his war.

PIZARRO. What King?

CHIEF. Holy Atahuallpa, Inca of earth and sky. His Kingdom is the widest in the world.

DE SOTO. How wide?

CHIEF. A man can run in it every day for a year.

DE SOTO. More than a thousand miles.

ESTETE. Poor savage, trying to impress us with his little
tribe.

PIZARRO. I think we've found more than a little tribe, Veedor. Tell me of this King. Who did he fight?

CHIEF. His brother Huascar. His father the great Inca
Huayana grew two sons. One by a wife, one by a not-wife.
At his death he cut the Kingdom in two for them. But
Atahuallpa wanted all. So he made war, and killed his
brother. Now he is lord of earth and sky.

PIZARRO. And he's the bastard?

All the INDIANS *cry out.*

Answer! He's the bastard?

CHIEF. He is Son of the Sun. He needs no wedded mother.
He is God.

INDIANS (*chanting*). Sapa Inca! Inca Capac!

PIZARRO. God?

CHIEF. God.

PIZARRO. God on earth?

VALVERDE. Christ defend us!

DE SOTO. Do you believe this?

13

CHIEF. It is true. The sun is God. Atahuallpa is his child sent to shine on us for a few years of life. Then he will return to his father's palace and live for ever.

PIZARRO. God on earth!

VALVERDE. Oh, my brothers, where have we come? The land of Anti-Christ! Do your duty, Spaniards! Take each an Indian and work to shift his soul. Go to them. Show them rigour! No softness to gentle idolatry. (*To the* INDIANS) The cross, you pagan dust!

They try to escape.

Stay them!

The SPANIARDS *ring them with swords.*

Repeat. Jesus Christ Inca!

INDIANS (*uncertainly*). Jesus Christ Inca!

ESTETE. Jesus Christ Inca!

INDIANS. Jesus Christ Inca!

The soldiers herd them off stage. Their cries punctuate the end of the scene. All go off after them, save PIZARRO *and* DE SOTO.

ATAHUALLPA. He surely is a god. He teaches my people to praise him.

PIZARRO. He's a god all right. They're scared to hell of him. And a bastard too. That's civil war – bastards against bastards!

ATAHUALLPA. I will see him. Let no one harm these men.

PIZARRO. Let's see you, then. What's it look like to be Son of the Sun?

DE SOTO. That's something in Europe no one's ever dared call himself.

PIZARRO. God on earth, living for ever!

DE SOTO. He's got a shock coming.

He goes off.

PIZARRO. Do you hear that, God? You're not going to like that! Because we've got a god worth a thousand of yours. A gentle God with gentle priests, and a couple of big cannon to blow you out of the sky!

VALVERDE (*off*) Jesus Christ Inca!

PIZARRO. Christ the Merciful, with his shackles and stakes!

So enjoy yourself while you can. Have a glorious shine.
(*He makes the sign of the cross*). Take that, Anti-Christ!
He runs off, laughing.

VALVERDE (*off*). Jesus Christ Inca!

INDIANS (*off*) *Cry out.*

Enter VILLAC UMU *and* CHALLCUCHIMA.

VILLAC UMU. Your people groan.

ATAHUALLPA. They groan with my voice.

CHALLCUCHIMA. Your people weep.

ATAHUALLPA. They weep with my tears.

CHALLCUCHIMA. He searches all the houses. He seeks
your crown. Remember the prophecy! The twelfth Lord
of the Four Quarters shall be the last. Inca, ware you!

VILLAC UMU. Inca, ware you!

ATAHUALLPA (*To* CHALLCUCHIMA) Go to him. Take
him my word. Tell him to greet me at Cajamarca, behind
the great mountains. If he is a god he will find me. If he
is no god, he will die.

Lights down on him. Priest and noblemen retire.

V

Night. Wild bird cries. DOMINGO *and* VASCA *on sentry
duty.*

VASCA. There must be a pissing thousand of 'em, every
night we halt.

DOMINGO. Why don't they just come and get us?

VASCA. They're waiting.

DOMINGO. What for?

VASCA. Maybe they're cannibals and there's a feast day
coming up.

DOMINGO. Very funny ... Six weeks in this pissing forest
and not one smell of gold. I think we've been had.

VASKA. Unless they're hiding it, like the General says.

DOMINGO. I don't believe it. God damned place. I'm starting
to rust.

VASCA. We all are. It's the damp. Another week and we'll have to get the blacksmith to cut us out.

Enter ESTETE *with* DE CANDIA *carrying an arquebus.*

VASCA. Who's there?

DE CANDIA. Talk on duty again and *I'll* cut you out.

DOMINGO. Yes, sir.

VASCA. Yes, sir.

They separate and go off.

DE CANDIA. They're right. Everything's rusting. Even you, my darling. (*The gun*) Look at her, Strozzi's most perfect model. She can stop a horse at five hundred paces. You're too good for brownies, my sweet.

ESTETE. What are they waiting for? Why don't they just attack and be done with it?

DE CANDIA. They'd find nothing against them. A hundred and eighty terrified men, nine of these and two cannon. If your King wasn't so mean we might just stand a chance out here.

ESTETE. Hold your tongue, De Candia.

DE CANDIA. Good: loyalty. That's what I like to see. The only thing that puzzles me is what the hell you get out of it. They tell me Royal Overseers get nothing.

ESTETE. Any man without self-interest must puzzle a Venetian. If you serve a King you must kill personal ambition. Only then can you become a channel between the people and its collective glory – which otherwise it would never feel. In Byzantium Court Officials were castrated to resemble the Order of Angels. But I don't expect you to understand.

DE CANDIA. You Spaniards! You men with missions! You just can't bear to think of yourselves as the thieves you are.

ESTETE. How dare you, sir!

Enter PIZARRO *and* YOUNG MARTIN.

DE CANDIA. Our noble General. They say in the Indies he traded his immortal part to the Devil.

ESTETE. For what, pray? Health? Breeding? Handsomeness?

DE CANDIA. That they don't tell.

ESTETE. I daresay not. I only wonder His Majesty could give command to such a man. I believe he's mad.

DE CANDIA No, but still dangerous.

ESTETE. What do you mean?

DE CANDIA. I've served under many men: but this is the first who makes me afraid. Look into him and you'll see a kind of death.

Bird cries fill the forest.

PIZARRO. Listen to them. That's the world. The eagle rips the condor; the condor rips the crow. And the crow would blind all the eagles in the sky if once it had the beak to do it. The clothed hunt the naked; the legitimates hunt the bastards, and put down the word Gentlemen to blot up the blood. Your Chivalry rules don't govern me, Martin. They're for belonging birds – like them: legitimate birds with claws trim on the perch their feathers left to them. Make no error; if I could once peck them off it, I'd tear them into gobbets to feed cats. Don't ever trust me, boy.

YOUNG MARTIN. Sir? I'm your man.

PIZARRO. Don't ever trust me.

YOUNG MARTIN. Sir?

PIZARRO. Or if you must, never say I deceived you. Know me.

YOUNG MARTIN. I do, sir. You are all I ever want to be.

PIZARRO. I am nothing you could ever want to be, or any man alive. Believe this: if the time ever came for you to harry me, I'd rip you too, easy as look at you. Because you belong too, Martin.

YOUNG MARTIN. I belong to you, sir!

PIZARRO. You belong to hope. To faith. To priests and pretences. To dipping flags and ducking heads; to laying hands and licking rings; to powers and parchments; and the whole vast stupid congregation of crowners and cross-kissers. You're a worshipper. Martin. A groveller. You were born with feet but you prefer your knees. It's you who make Bishops – Kings – Generals. You trust me, I'll hurt you past believing. (*A pause*) Have the sentries changed?

YOUNG MARTIN. Not yet, sir.

PIZARRO. Little Lord of Hope, I'm harsh with you. You own everything I've lost. I despise the keeping, and I loathe the losing. Where can a man live, between two hates?

He goes towards the two officers.

Gentlemen.

ESTETE. How is your wound tonight, General?

PIZARRO. The calmer for your inquiring, Veedor.

DE CANDIA. Well, and what's your plan, sir?

PIZARRO. To go on until I'm stopped.

DE CANDIA. Admirable simplicity.

ESTETE. What kind of plan is that?

PIZARRO. You have a better? It's obvious they've been ordered to hold off.

ESTETE. Why?

PIZARRO. If it's wickedness I'm sure the crown can guess it as soon as the Army.

ESTETE. Sir, I know your birth hasn't fitted for much civility, but remember, in me speaks your King.

PIZARRO. Well, go and write to him. Set down more about my unfitness in your report. Then show it to the birds.

He goes off. ESTETE *goes off another way.* DE CANDIA *laughs and follows him.*

VI

Light brightens to morning.
Enter OLD MARTIN.

OLD MARTIN. We were in the forest for six weeks, but at last we escaped and found on the other side our first witness of a great empire. There was a road fifteen feet wide, bordered with mimosa and blue glories, with walls on both sides the height of a man. We rode it for days, six horses abreast: and all the way, far up the hillsides, were huge fields of corn laid out in terraces, and a net of water in a thousand canals. (*Exit*)

    Lights up on ATAHUALLPA, *above.*

MANCO. Manco your Chasqui speaks. They move on the road to Ricaplaya.

ATAHUALLPA. What do they do?

MANCO. They walk through the field terraces. They listen to toil-songs. They clap their hands at fields of llama.

    Enter groups of INDIANS, *singing a toil-song and miming their work of sowing and reaping.* PIZARRO, *the* PRIESTS, FELIPILLO *and* SOLDIERS, *among them* DE SOTO, DE CANDIA, DIEGO, ESTETE *and* YOUNG MARTIN, *enter and stand watching.* YOUNG MARTIN *carries a drum.*

DE NIZZA. How beautiful their tongue sounds.

YOUNG MARTIN. I'm trying to study it but it's very hard. All the words seem to slip together.

FELIPILLO. Oh, very hard, yes. But more hard for Indian to learn Spanish.

DE NIZZA. I'm sure. See how contented they look.

DIEGO. It's the first time I've ever seen people glad at working.

DE SOTO. This is their Headman.

PIZARRO. You are the Lord of the Manor?

FELIPILLO *interprets.*

HEADMAN. Here all work together in families: fifty, a hundred, a thousand. I am head of a thousand families. I give out to all food. I give out to all clothes. I give out to all confessing.

DE NIZZA. Confessing?

HEADMAN. I have priest power . . . I confess my people of all crimes against the laws of the sun.

DE NIZZA. What laws are these?

HEADMAN. It is the seventh month. That is why they must pick corn.

ATAHUALLPA (*intoning*) In the eighth month you will plough. In the ninth, sow maize. In the tenth, mend your roofs.

HEADMAN. Each age also has its tasks.

ATAHUALLPA. Nine years to twelve, protect harvests. Twelve to eighteen, care for herds. Eighteen to twenty-five, warriors for me – Atahuallpa Inca!

FELIPILLO. They are stupid; always do what they are told.

DE SOTO. This is because they are poor?

FELIPILLO. Not poor. Not rich. All same.

ATAHUALLPA. At twenty-five all will marry. All will receive one tupu of land.

HEADMAN. What may be covered by one hundred pounds of maize.

ATAHUALLPA. They will never move from there. At birth of a son one more tupu will be given. At birth of a daughter, half a tupu. At fifty all people will leave work for ever and be fed in honour till they die.

DE SOTO. I have settled several lands. This is the first I've entered which shames our Spain.

ESTETE. Shames?

PIZARRO. Oh, it's not difficult to shame Spain. Here shames every country which teaches we are born greedy for possessions. Clearly we're made greedy when we're assured it's natural. But there's a picture for a Spanish eye! There's nothing to covet, so covetousness dies at birth.

DE SOTO. But don't you have any nobles or grand people?

HEADMAN. The King has great men near him to order the country. But they are few.

DE SOTO. How then can he make sure so many are happy over so large a land?

HEADMAN. His messengers run light and dark, one after one, over four great roads. No one else may move on them. So he has eyes everywhere. He sees you now.

PIZARRO. Now?

ATAHUALLPA. Now!

CHALLCUCHIMA *enters with* MANCO, *bearing the image of the Sun on a pole.*

CHALLCUCHIMA. I bring greeting from Atahuallpa Inca, Lord of the Four Quarters, King of the earth and sky.

ESTETE. I will speak with him. A King's man must always

greet a King's man. We bring greeting from King Carlos, Emperor of Spain and Austria. We bring blessing from Jesus Christ, the Son of God.

ATAHUALLPA. Blessing!

CHALLCUCHIMA. *I* am sent by the son of God. He orders *you* to visit him.

ESTETE. Orders? Does he take us for servants?

CHALLCUCHIMA. All men are his servants.

ESTETE. Does he think so? He's got awakening coming.

CHALLCUCHIMA. Awakening?

PIZARRO. Veedor, under pardon, let my peasant tongue have a word. Where is your King?

CHALLCUCHIMA. Cajamarca. Behind the great mountains. Perhaps they are too high for you.

ESTETE. There isn't a hill in your whole country a Spaniard couldn't climb in full armour.

CHALLCUCHIMA. That is wonderful.

PIZARRO. How long should we march before we find him?

CHALLCUCHIMA. One life of Mother Moon.

FELIPILLO. A month.

PIZARRO. For us, two weeks. Tell him we come.

ATAHUALLPA. He gives his word with no fear.

CHALLCUCHIMA. Ware you! It is great danger to take back your word.

PIZARRO. I do not fear danger. What I say I do.

CHALLCUCHIMA. So. Do.

   CHALLCUCHIMA *and* MANCO *go off.*

ATAHUALLPA. He speaks with a God's tongue. Let us take his blessing.

DE SOTO. Well, God help us now.

DE CANDIA. He'd better. I don't know who else will get us out of this. Certainly not the artillery.

FELIPILLO (*imitating* CHALCUCHIMA'S *walk and voice*). So! Do.

DE SOTO. Be still. You're too free.

ESTETE. My advice to you now is to wait for the reinforcements.

PIZARRO. I thank you for it.

DE SOTO. There's no telling when they'll come, sir. We daren't stay till then.

PIZARRO. But *you* of course will.

ESTETE. I?

PIZARRO. I cannot hazard the life of a Royal officer.

ESTETE. My personal safety has never concerned me, General. My Master's service is all I care for.

PIZARRO. That's why we must ensure its continuance. I'll give you twenty men. You can make a garrison.

ESTETE. I must decline, General. If you go – I go also.

PIZARRO. I'm infinitely moved, Veedor – but my orders remain. You stay here. (*To his page*) Call Assembly.

YOUNGMARTIN (*banging his drum*). Assembly! Assembly!

VII

The Company pelts on. ESTETE *goes off angrily.*

PIZARRO. We are commanded to court by a brown King, more powerful than any you have ever heard of, sole owner of all the gold we came for. We have three roads. Go back, and he kills us. Stay here, and he kills us. Go on, and he still may kill us. Who fears to meet him can stay here with the Veedor and swell a garrison. He'll have no disgrace, but no gold neither. Who stirs?

RODAS. Well, I pissing stir for once. I'm not going to be chewed up by no bloody heathen king. What do you say, Vasca lad?

VASCA. I don't know. I reckon if he chews us first, he chews you second. We're the eggs and you're the stew.

RODAS. Ha, ha, day of a hundred jokes!

SALINAS. Come on friend, for God's sake. Who's going to sew us up if you desert?

RODAS. You can all rot for all I care, breeches and what's bloody in 'em.

SALINAS. Bastard!

RODAS. To hell with the lot of you! (*He walks off*)

PIZARRO. Anyone else?

DOMINGO. Well, I don't know . . . Maybe he's right.

JUAN. Hey, Pedro, what do you think?

PEDRO. Hell, no! Vasca's right. It's as safe to go as stay here.

SALINAS. That's right.

VASCA. Anyway, I didn't come to keep no pissing garrison.

PEDRO. Nor me. I'm going on.

JUAN. Right boy.

SALINAS. And me.

DOMINGO. Well, I don't know . . .

VASCA. Oh, close your mouth. You're like a pissing girl. (*To* PIZARRO.) We're coming. Just find us the gold.

PIZARRO. All right then. (*To* YOUNG MARTIN) You stay here.

YOUNG MARTIN. No, sir. The place of a squire is at all times by his Knight's side. Laws of Chivalry.

PIZARRO (*touched*). Get them in rank. *Move!*

YOUNG MARTIN. Company in rank. Move!

The soldiers form up in rank.

PIZARRO. Stand firm. Firmer! . . . Look at you, you could be dead already. If he sees you like that you will be. Make no error, he's watching every step you take. You're not men any longer, you're Gods now. Eternal Gods, each one of you. Two can play this immortality game, my lads. I want to see you move over his land like figures from a Lent Procession. He must see Gods walk on earth. Indifferent! Uncrushable! No death to be afraid of. I tell you, one shiver dooms the lot of us. One yelp of fright and we'll never be heard of again. He'll serve us like cheese-worms you crush with a knife. So come on you tattered trash – shake out the straw. Forget your village magic: fingers in crosses, saints under your shirts. You can grant prayers now – no need to answer them. Come on! Fix your eyes! Follow the pig-boy to his glory! I'll have an Empire for my farm. A million boys driving in the pigs at night. And each one of you will own a share – juicy black earth a hundred mile apiece – and golden ploughs to cut it! Get up you God-boys – March!

MARTIN *bangs his drum. The Spaniards begin to march in slow motion. Above, masked Indians move on to the upper level.*

MANCO. They move Inca! they come! One hundred and sixty and seven.

ATAHUALLPA. Where?

MANCO. Zaran.

VILLAC UMU. Ware! Ware, Inca!

MANCO. They move all in step. Not fast, not slow. They keep straight on from dark to dark.

VILLAC UMU. Ware! Ware, Inca.

MANCO. They are at Motupe, Inca! They do not look on left or right.

VILLAC UMU. Ware! this is great danger.

ATAHUALLPA. No danger. He is coming to bless me. A god and all his priests. Praise Father Sun!

ALL ABOVE (*chanting*). Viracochian Aticsi.

ATAHUALLPA. Praise Sapa Inca!

ALL ABOVE. Sapa Inca! Inca Capac!

ATAHUALLPA. Praise Inti Cori.

ALL ABOVE. Caylla int'i cori.

CHALLCUCHIMA. They come to the mountains.

VILLAC UMU. Kill them now.

ATAHUALLPA. Praise Atahuallpa.

VILLAC UMU. Destroy them! Teach them death!

ATAHUALLPA. Praise Atahuallpa!

ALL ABOVE. Atahuallpa! Sapa Inca! Huaccha Cuyak!

ATAHUALLPA. Let them see my mountains!

A crash of primitive instruments. The lights snap out and, lit from the side, the rays of the metal sun throw long shadows across the wooden wall. All the Spaniards fall down. A cold blue light fills the stage.

DE SOTO. God in heaven!

Enter OLD MARTIN.

OLD MARTIN. You call them the Andes. Picture a curtain of stone hung by some giant across your path. Mountains set on mountains: cliffs on cliffs. Hands of rock a hundred yards high, with flashing nails where the snow never moved, scratching the gashed face of the sun. For miles around the jungle lay black in its shadow. A freezing cold fell on us.

PIZARRO. Up, my godlings. Up, my little gods. Take heart, now. He's watching you. *Get to your feet!* (*To* DIEGO) Master, what of the horses?

DIEGO. D'you need them sir?

PIZARRO. They're vital, boy.

DIEGO. Then you'll have 'em, sir. They'll follow you as we will.

PIZARRO. Up we go, then! We're coming for you, Atahuallpa. Show me the toppest peak-top you can pile – show me the lid of the world – I'll stand tiptoe on it and pull you right out of the sky. I'll grab you by the legs, you Son of the Sun, and smash your flaming crown on the rocks. Bless them, Church!

VALVERDE. God stay you, and stay with you all.

DE NIZZA. Amen.

Whilst PIZARRO *is calling his last speech to the Inca, the silent King thrice beckons to him, and retires backwards out of the sun into blackness. In the cold light there now ensues:*

VIII

THE MIME OF THE GREAT ASCENT

As OLD MARTIN *describes their ordeal, the men climb the Andes. It is a terrible progress; a stumbling, tortuous climb into the clouds, over ledges and giant chasms, performed to an eerie, cold music made from the thin whine of huge saws.*

OLD MARTIN. Have you ever climbed a mountain in full armour? That's what we did, him going first the whole way up a tiny path into the clouds, with drops sheer on both sides into nothing. For hours we crept forward like blind men, the sweat freezing on our faces, lugging skittery leak-

ing horses, and pricked all the time for the ambush that
would tip us into death. Each turn of the path it grew
colder. The friendly trees of the forest dropped away, and
there were only pines. Then they went too, and there were
just scrubby little bushes standing up in ice. All round us
the rocks began to whine with cold. And always above us,
or below us, those filthy condor birds, hanging on the air
with great tasselled wings.

*It grows darker. The music grows colder yet. The men
freeze and hang their heads for a long moment, before resuming their desperate climb.*

Then night. We lay down twos and threes together on the
path, and hugged like lovers for warmth in that burning
cold. And most cried. We got up with cold iron for bones
and went on. Four days like that; groaning, not speaking;
the breath a blade in our lungs. Four days, slowly, like flies
on a wall; limping flies, dying flies, up an endless wall of
rock. A tiny army lost in the creases of the moon.

INDIANS (*off: in echo*). Stand!

The Spaniards whirl round. VILLAC UMU *and his
attendants appear, clothed entirely in white fur. The
High Priest wears a snow-white llama head on top of
his own.*

VILLAC UMU. You see Villac Umu. Chief Priest of the Sun.
Why do you come?

PIZARRO. To see the Great Inca.

VILLAC UMU. Why will you see him?

PIZARRO. To give him blessing.

VILLAC UMU. Why will you bless him?

PIZARRO. He is a God. I am a God.

VALVERDE (*sotto voce*). General!

PIZARRO. Be still.

VILLAC UMU. Below you is the town of Cajamarca. The
great Inca orders: rest there. Tomorrow early he will come
to you. Do not move from the town. Outside it is his anger.

He goes off with his attendants.

VALVERDE. What have you done, sir?

PIZARRO. Sent him news to amaze him.

26

VALVERDE. I cannot approve blasphemy.

PIZARRO. To conquer for Christ, one can surely usurp his name for a night, Father. Set on.

IX

A dreary light.
The Spaniards fan out over the stage. DE SOTO *goes off.*

OLD MARTIN. So down we went from ledge to ledge, and out on to a huge plain of eucalyptus trees, all glowing in the failing light. And there, at the other end, lay a vast white town with roofs of straw. As night fell, we entered it. We came into an empty square, larger than any in Spain. All round it ran long white buildings, three times the height of a man. Everywhere was grave quiet. You could almost touch the silence. Up on the hill we could see the Inca's tents, and the lights from his fires ringing the valley. (*Exit.*)
Some sit. All look up at the hillside.

DIEGO. How many do you reckon there's up there?

DE CANDIA. Ten thousand.

DE SOTO (*re-entering*). The town's empty. Not even a dog.

DOMINGO. It's a trap. I know it's a trap.

PIZARRO. Felipillo! Where's that little rat? Felipillo!

FELIPILLO. General, Lord.

PIZARRO. What does this mean?

FELIPILLO. I don't know. Perhaps it is order of welcome. Great people. Much honour.

VALVERDE. Nonsense, it's a trick, a brownie trick. He's got us all marked for death.

DE NIZZA. He could have killed us at any time. Why should he take such trouble with us?

PIZARRO. Because we're Gods, Father. He'll change soon enough when he finds out different.

DE SOTO. Brace up, boy! It's what you came for, isn't it? Death and glory?

YOUNG MARTIN. Yes, sir.

PIZARRO. De Soto. De Candia. (*They go to him*) It's got to be ambush. That's our only hope.

DE SOTO. Round the square?

PIZARRO. Lowers the odds. Three thousand at most.

DE CANDIA. Thirty to one. Not low enough.

PIZARRO. It'll have to do. We're not fighting ten thousand or three. One man: that's all. Get him, the rest collapse.

DE SOTO. Even if we can, they'll kill us all to get him back.

PIZARRO. If there's a knife at his throat? It's a risk, sure. But what do worshippers do when you snatch their God?

DE CANDIA. Pray to you instead.

DIEGO. It's wonderful. Grab the King, grab the Kingdom!

DE NIZZA. It would avoid bloodshed.

PIZARRO. What do you say?

DE CANDIA. It's the only way. It could work.

DE SOTO. With God's help.

PIZARRO. Then pray all. Disperse. Light fires. Make confession. Battle orders at first light.

Most disperse. Some lie down to pray and sleep.

DE NIZZA (*to* DE CANDIA). Shall I hear your confession now, my son?

DE CANDIA. You'd best save all that for tomorrow, Father. For the men who are left. What have we got to confess tonight but thoughts of murder?

DE NIZZA. Then confess those.

DE CANDIA. Why? Should I feel shame for them? What would I say to God if I refused to destroy His enemies?

VALVERDE. More Venetian nonsense!

DE NIZZA. God has no enemies, my son. Only those nearer to Him or farther from Him.

DE CANDIA. Well, my job is to aim at the far ones. I'll go and position the guns. Excuse me.

He goes off.

PIZARRO. Diego, look to the horses. I know they're sorry, but we'll need them brisk.

VALVERDE. Come my brother, we'll pray together.

They go too.

PIZARRO. The cavalry will split and hide in the buildings, there and there.

DE SOTO. And the infantry in file – there, and round there.

PIZARRO. Perfect. Herrada can command one flank, de Barbaran the other. Everyone hidden.

DE SOTO. They'll suspect then.

PIZARRO. No, the Church will greet them.

DE SOTO. We'll need a watchword.

PIZARRO. San Jago.

DE SOTO. San Jago. Good.

The old man comes upon his page, who is sitting huddled by himself.

PIZARRO. Are you scared?

YOUNG MARTIN. No, sir. Yes, sir.

PIZARRO. You're a good boy. If ever we get out of this, I'll make you a gift of whatever you ask me. Is that chivalrous enough for you?

YOUNG MARTIN. Being your page is enough, sir.

PIZARRO. And there's nothing else you want?

YOUNG MARTIN. A sword, sir.

PIZARRO. Of course . . . Take what rest you can. Call Assembly at first light.

YOUNG MARTIN. Yes, sir. Good night sir.

DE SOTO. Good night, Martin. Try and sleep.

The boy lies down to sleep. The singing of prayers is heard, off, all around.

PIZARRO. Hope, lovely hope. A sword's no mere bar of metal for him. His world still has sacred objects. How remote . . .

DIEGO. Holy Virgin, give us victory. If you do, I'll make you a present of a fine Indian cloak. But you let us down, and I'll leave you for the Virgin of the Conception, and I mean that.

He lies down also. The prayers die away. Silence.

X

Semi-darkness.

PIZARRO. This is probably our last night. If we die, what will we have gone for?

DE SOTO. Spain. Christ.

PIZARRO. I envy you, Cavalier.

DE SOTO. For what?

PIZARRO. Your service. God. King. It's all simple for you.

DE SOTO. No, sir, it's not simple. But it's what I've chosen.

PIZARRO. Yes. And what have I chosen?

DE SOTO. To be a King yourself. Or as good, if we win here.

PIZARRO. And what's that at my age? Not only swords turn into bars of metal. Sceptres too. What's left, De Soto?

DE SOTO. What you told me in Spain. A name for ballads. The man of Honour has three good lives: The Life Today. The Life to Come. The Life of Fame.

PIZARRO. Fame is long. Death is longer . . . Does anyone ever die for anything? I thought so once. Life was fierce with feeling. It was all hope, like on that boy. Swords shone and armour sang, and cheese bit you, and kissing burned and Death – ah, death was going to make an exception in my case. I couldn't believe I was ever going to die. But once you know it – really know it – it's all over. You know you've been cheated, and nothing's the same again.

DE SOTO. Cheated?

PIZARRO. Time cheats us all the way. Children, yes – having children goes some steps to defeating it. Nothing else. It would have been good to have a son.

DE SOTO. Did you never think to marry?

PIZARRO. With my parentage? The only women who would have had me weren't the sort you married. Spain's a pile of horsedung . . . When I began to think of a world here, something in me was longing for a new place like a country after rain, washed clear of all the badges and barriers, the pebbles men drop to tell them where they are

on a plain that's got no landmarks. I used to look after
women with hope, but they didn't have much time for me.
One of them said – what was it? – my soul was frostbitten.
That's a word for you – Frostbitten. How goes it, man?

VASCA (*off*). A clear night, sir. Everything clear.

PIZARRO. I had a girl once, on a rock by the Southern
Ocean. I lay with her one afternoon in winter, wrapped
up in her against the cold, and the sea-fowl screaming,
and it was the best hour of my life. I felt then that sea-
water and bird droppings and the little pits in human flesh
were all linked together for some great end right out of
the net of words to catch. Not just my words, but anyone's.
Then I lost it. Time came back. For always.

He moves away, feeling his side.

DE SOTO. Does it pain you?

PIZARRO. Oh, yes: *that's* still fierce.

DE SOTO. You should try to sleep. We'll need our strength.

PIZARRO. Listen, listen! Everything we feel is made of
Time. All the beauties of life are shaped by it. Imagine a
fixed sunset: the last note of a song that hung an hour,
or a kiss for half of it. Try and halt a moment in our lives
and it becomes maggoty at once. Even that word 'moment'
is wrong, since that would mean a speck of time, something
you could pick up on a rag and peer at . . . But that's the
awful trap of life. You can't escape maggots unless you
go with Time, and if you go, they wriggle in you anyway.

DE SOTO. This is gloomy talk.

YOUNG MARTIN *groans in his sleep.*

PIZARRO. For a gloomy time. You were talking women. I
loved them with all the juice in me – but oh, the cheat in
that tenderness. What is it but a lust to own their beauty,
not them, which you never can: like trying to own the
beauty of a goblet by paying for it. And even if you could
it would become you and get soiled . . . I'm an old man,
Cavalier, I can explain nothing. What I mean is: Time
whipped up the lust in me and Time purged it. I was
dandled on Time's knee and made to gurgle, then put

31

to my sleep. I've been cheated from the moment I was born because there's death in everything.

DE SOTO. Except in God.

A pause.

PIZARRO. When I was young, I used to sit on the slope outside the village and watch the sun go down, and I used to think: if only I could find the place where it sinks to rest for the night, I'd find the source of life, like the beginning of a river. I used to wonder what it could be like. Perhaps an island, a strange place of white sand, where the people never died. Never grew old, or felt pain, and never died.

DE SOTO. Sweet fancy.

PIZARRO. It's what your mind runs to when it lacks instruction. If I had a son, I'd kill him if he didn't read his book. . . . Where does the sun rest at night?

DE SOTO. Nowhere. It's a heavenly body sent by God to move round the earth in perpetual motion.

PIZARRO. Do you know this?

DE SOTO. All Europe knows it.

PIZARRO. What if they were wrong? If it settled here each evening, somewhere in those great mountains, like a God laid down to sleep? To a savage mind it must make a fine God. I myself can't fix anything nearer to a thought of worship than standing at dawn and watching it fill the world. Like the coming of something eternal, against going flesh. What a fantastic wonder that anyone on earth should dare to say: 'That's my father. My father: the sun!' It's silly – but tremendous . . . You know – strange nonsense: since first I heard of him I've dreamed of him every night. A black king with glowing eyes, sporting the sun for a crown. What does it mean?

DE SOTO. I've no skill with dreams. Perhaps a soothsayer would tell you: 'The Inca's your enemy. You dream his emblem to increase your hate.'

PIZARRO. But I feel no enemy.

DE SOTO. Surely you do.

PIZARRO. No. Only that of all meetings I have made in my

life, this with him is the one I have to make. Maybe it's my death. Or maybe new life. I feel just this: all my days have been a path to this one morning.

OLD MARTIN. The sixteenth of November 1532. First light, sir.

XI

Lights brighten slowly.

VALVERDE (*singing, off*). Exsurge Domine.
SOLDIERS (*singing in unison*). Exsurge Domine.
    All the company comes on, chanting.
VALVERDE. Deus meus eripe me de manu peccatoris.
SOLDIERS. Deus meus eripe me de manu peccatoris.
    All kneel, spread across the stage.
VALVERDE. Many strong bulls have compassed me.
DE NIZZA. They have gaped upon me with their mouths, as a lion ravening.
VALVERDE. I am poured out like water, and all my bones are scattered.
DE NIZZA. My heart is like wax, melting in the midst of my bowels. My tongue cleaves to my jaws, and thou hast brought me into the dust of death.
    All freeze.
OLD MARTIN. The dust of death. It was in our noses. The full scare came to us quickly, like plague.
    All heads turn.
The men were crammed in buildings all round the square.
    All stand.
They stood there shivering, making water where they stood. An hour went by. Two. Three.
    All remain absolutely still.
Five. Not a move from the Indian camp. Not a sound from us. Only the weight of the day. A hundred and sixty men in full armour, cavalry mounted, infantry at the ready, standing in dead silence – glued in a trance of waiting.

PIZARRO. Hold fast now. Come on – you're Gods. Take heart. Don't blink your eyes, that's too much noise.

OLD MARTIN. Seven.

PIZARRO. Stiff. Stiff. You're your own masters, boys. Not peasant anymore. This is your time. Own it. Live it.

OLD MARTIN. Nine. Ten hours passed. There were few of us then who didn't feel the cold begin to crawl.

PIZARRO (*whispering*). Send him, send him, send him, send him.

OLD MARTIN. Dread comes with the evening air. Even the priest's arm fails.

PIZARRO. The sun's going out!

OLD MARTIN. No one looks at his neighbour. Then, with the shadow of night already running towards us—

YOUNG MARTIN. *They're coming!* Look, down the hill—

DE SOTO. How many?

YOUNG MARTIN. Hundreds, sir.

DE CANDIA. Thousands – two or three.

PIZARRO. Can you see *him*?

DE CANDIA. No, not yet.

DOMINGO. What's that – out there in front – they're doing something.

VASCA. Looks like sweeping—

DIEGO. They're sweeping the road!

DOMINGO. For *him*! They're sweeping the road for him! Five hundred of 'em sweeping the road!

SALINAS. God in Heaven!

PIZARRO. Are they armed?

DE CANDIA. To the teeth!

DE SOTO. How?—

DE CANDIA. Axes and spears.

YOUNG MARTIN. They're all glittering, glittering red!—

DIEGO. It's the sun! Like someone's stabbed it!—

VASCA. Squirting blood all over the sky!

DOMINGO. It's an omen!—

SALINAS. Shut up.

DOMINGO. It must be. The whole country's bleeding. Look for yourself. It's an omen!

VALVERDE. This is the day foretold you by the Angel of the Apocalypse. Satan reigns on the altars, jeering at the true God. The earth teems with corrupt kings.

DOMINGO. Oh God! Oh God! Oh God! Oh God!

DE SOTO. Control yourself!

DE CANDIA. They're stopping!

YOUNG MARTIN. They're throwing things down, sir!

PIZARRO. What things?

DE CANDIA. Weapons.

PIZARRO. No!

DIEGO. Yes, sir. I can see. All their weapons. They're throwing them down in a pile.

VASCA. They're laying down their arms.

SALINAS. I don't believe it!

VASCA. They are. They are leaving everything!

DOMINGO. It's a miracle.

DE SOTO. Why? *Why?*

PIZARRO. Because we're Gods. You see? You don't approach Gods with weapons.

Strange music faintly in the distance. Through all the ensuing it grows louder and louder.

DE SOTO. What's that?

YOUNG MARTIN. It's *him*. He's coming, sir.

PIZARRO. Where?

YOUNG MARTIN. *There,* sir.

DIEGO. Oh, look, *look.* God Almighty, it's not happening! ...

DE SOTO. Steady man.

PIZARRO. You're coming. Come on then! *Come on!*

DE SOTO. General, it's time to hide.

PIZARRO. Yes, quick now. No one must be seen but the priests. Out there in the middle, Fathers: everyone else in hiding.

DE SOTO. Quick! jump to it!

Only now do the men break, scatter and vanish.

PIZARRO (*to* YOUNG MARTIN). You too.

YOUNG MARTIN. Until the fighting, sir?

PIZARRO. All the time for you, fighting or no.

YOUNG MARTIN. Oh no, sir!

35

PIZARRO. Do as I say. Take him, de Soto.

DE SOTO. Save you, General.

PIZARRO. And you, de Soto. San Jago!

DE SOTO. San Jago! Come on.

DE CANDIA. There are seven gunners on the roof. And three over there.

PIZARRO. Watch the cross-fire.

DE CANDIA. I'll wait for your signal.

PIZARRO. Then sound yours.

DE CANDIA. You'll hear it.

PIZARRO (*to* FELIPILLO). Felipillo! Stand there! Now . . . now . . . NOW!

    He hurries off.

XII

The music crashes over the stage as the Indian procession enters in an astonishing explosion of colour. The King's attendants – many of them playing musical instruments: reed pipes, cymbals, and giant marraccas – are as gay as parrots. They wear costumes of orange and yellow, and fantastic headdresses of gold and feathers, with eyes embossed on them in staring black enamel. By contrast, ATAHUALLPA INCA presents a picture of utter simplicity. He is dressed from head to foot in white: across his eyes is a mask of jade mosaic, and round his head a circlet of plain gold. Silence falls. The King glares about him.

ATAHUALLPA (*haughtily*). Where is the God?

VALVERDE (*through* FELIPILLO). I am a Priest of God.

ATAHUALLPA. I do not want the priest. I want the God. Where is he? He sent me greeting.

VALVERDE. That was our General. Our God cannot be seen.

ATAHUALLPA. *I* may see him.

VALVERDE. No. He was killed by men and went into the sky.

ATAHUALLPA. A God cannot be killed. See my father. You cannot kill him. He lives for ever and looks over his children every day.

VALVERDE. I am the answer to all mysteries. Hark, pagan and I will expound.

OLD MARTIN. And so he did, from the Creation to Our Lord's ascension.

He goes off.

VALVERDE (*walking among the Indians to the right*). And when he went he left the Pope as Regent for him.

DE NIZZA (*walking among the Indians to the left*). And when he went he left the Pope as Regent for him.

VALVERDE. He has commanded our King to bring all men to belief in the true God.

VALVERDE
DE NIZZA (*together*) In Christ's name therefore I charge you: yield yourself his willing vassal.

ATAHUALLPA. I am the vassal of no man. I am the greatest Prince on earth. Your King is great. He has sent you far across the water. So he is my brother. But your Pope is mad. He gives away countries that are not his. His faith also is mad.

VALVERDE. Beware!

ATAHUALLPA. Ware you! You kill my people; you make them slaves. By what power?

VALVERDE. By this. (*He offers a Bible*) The Word of God.

ATAHUALLPA *holds it to his ear. He listens intently. He shakes it.*

ATAHUALLPA. No word.

He smells the book, and then licks it. Finally he throws it down impatiently.

God is angry with your insults.

VALVERDE. Blasphemy!

ATAHUALLPA. God is angry.

VALVERDE. Francisco Pizarro, do you stay your hand when Christ is insulted? Let this pagan feel the power of your arm. I absolve you all! San Jago!

P I Z A R R O *appears above with drawn sword, and in a great voice sings out his battle-cry:*

PIZARRO. SAN JAGO Y CIERRA ESPANA!

Instantly from all sides the soldiers rush in, echoing the great cry.

SOLDIERS. SAN JAGO!

There is a tense pause. The Indians look at this ring of armed men in terror. A violent drumming begins, and there ensues:

THE MIME OF THE GREAT MASSACRE

To a savage music, wave upon wave of Indians are slaughtered and rise again to protect their lord who stands bewildered in their midst. It is all in vain. Relentlessly the Spanish soldiers hew their way through the ranks of feathered attendants towards their quarry. They surround him. S A L I N A S *snatches the crown off his head and tosses it up to* P I Z A R R O, *who catches it and to a great shout crowns himself. All the Indians cry out in horror. The drum hammers on relentlessly while* A T A H U A L L P A *is led off at sword-point by the whole band of Spaniards. At the same time, dragged from the middle of the sun by howling Indians, a vast bloodstained cloth bellies out over the stage. All rush off; their screams fill the theatre. The lights fade out slowly on the rippling cloth of blood.*

Act Two

I

Darkness. A bitter Inca lament is intoned, above.

Lights up a little. The bloodstained cloth still lies over the stage. In the sun chamber ATAHUALLPA *stands in chains, his back to the audience, his white robe dirty with blood. Although he is unmasked, we cannot yet see his face, only a tail of black hair hanging down his neck.*

OLD MARTIN *appears. From opposite,* YOUNG MARTIN *comes in, stumbling with shock. He collapses on his knees.*

OLD MARTIN. Look at the warrior where he struts. Glory on his sword. Salvation in his new spurs. One of the knights at last. The very perfect knight Sir Martin, tender in virtue, bodyguard of Christ Jesus, we are all eased out of kids' dreams; but who can be ripped out of them and live loving after? Three thousand Indians we killed in that square. The only Spaniard to be wounded was the General, scratched by a sword whilst protecting his Royal prisoner. That night, as I knelt vomiting into a canal, the empire of the Incas stopped. The spring of the clock was snapped. For a thousand miles men sat down not knowing what to do.

Enter DE SOTO.

DE SOTO. Well, boy, what is it? They weren't armed, is that it? If they had been we could be dead now.

YOUNG MARTIN. Honourably dead! Not alive and shamed.

DE SOTO. And Christ would be dead here too, scarcely born. When I first breathed blood it was in my lungs for days. But the time comes when you won't even sniff when it pours over your feet. See, boy, here and now it's kill or get killed. And if we go, we betray Christ, whose coming we are here to make.

YOUNG MARTIN. You talk as if we're butlers, sent to open the door for him.

DE SOTO. So we are.

YOUNG MARTIN. No! He's with us now – at all times – or never.

DE SOTO. He's with us, yes, but not with them. After he is, there will be time for mercy.

YOUNG MARTIN. When there is no danger! Some mercy!

DE SOTO. Would you put Christ in danger, then?

YOUNG MARTIN. He can look after himself.

DE SOTO. He can't. That's why he needs servants.

YOUNG MARTIN. To kill for him?

DE SOTO. If necessary. And it was. My parish priest used to say: There must always be dying to make new life. I think of that whenever I draw the sword. My constant thought is: I must be winter for Our Lord to be Spring.

YOUNG MARTIN. I don't understand.

PIZARRO *and* FELIPILLO *come in.*

PIZARRO. Stand up when the Second addresses you. What are you, a defiled girl? (*To* DE SOTO) I've sent de Candia back to the Garrison. Reinforcements should be there presently. Come now: let's meet this King.

II

Lights up more.

They move upstage and bow. Above, OELLO *and* INTI COUSSI *come in and kneel on either side of the Inca, who ignores the embassy below.*

My lord, I am Francisco Pizarro, General of Spain. It is an honour to speak with you. (*Pause*) You are very tall, my lord. In my country are no such tall men. (*Pause*) My lord, won't you speak?

ATAHUALLPA *turns. For the first time we see his face, carved in a mould of serene arrogance. His whole bearing displays the most entire dignity and*

natural grace. When he moves or speaks, it is always
with the consciousness of his divine origin, his
sacred function and his absolute power.

ATAHUALLPA (*to* FELIPILLO). Tell him I am Atahuallpa
Capac, Son of the Sun, Sun of the Moon, Lord of the
Four Quarters. Why does he not kneel?

FELIPILLO. The Inca says he wishes he had killed you when
you first came.

PIZARRO. Why didn't he?

ATAHUALLPA. He lied to me. He is not a God. I came
for blessing. He sharpened his knives on the shoulders
of my servants. I have no word for *him* whose word is
evil.

FELIPILLO. He says he wants to make slaves of your best
warriors, then kill all the others. Especially you he would
kill because you are old; no use as slave.

PIZARRO. Tell him he will live to rue those intentions.

FELIPILLO. You make my master angry. He will kill you
tomorrow. Then he will give that wife (*he indicates* OELLO)
to me for my pleasure.

OELLO *rises in alarm.*

ATAHUALLPA. How dare you speak this before my face?

YOUNG MARTIN. General.

PIZARRO. What?

YOUNG MARTIN. Excuse me, sir, but I don't think you're
being translated aright.

PIZARRO. You don't?

YOUNG MARTIN. No sir. Nor the King to you. I know a
little of the language and he said nothing about slaves.

PIZARRO. You! What are you saying?

FELIPILLO. General Lord. This boy know nothing how to
speak.

YOUNG MARTIN. I know more than you think. I know
you're lying . . . He's after the woman, General. I saw him
before, in the square, grabbing at her.

PIZARRO. Is that true?

YOUNG MARTIN. As I live, sir.

PIZARRO. What do you say?

FELIPILLO. General Lord, I speak wonderful for you. No one speak so wonderful.

PIZARRO. What about that girl?

FELIPILLO. You give her as present to me, yes?

PIZARRO. The Inca's wife?

FELIPILLO. Inca has many wives. This one small, not famous.

PIZARRO. Get out.

FELIPILLO. General Lord!

PIZARRO. You work another trick like this and I'll swear I'll hang you. Out!

    FELIPILLO *spits at him and runs off.*

PIZARRO. Could you take his place?

YOUNG MARTIN. With work, sir.

PIZARRO. Work, then. Come, let's make a start. Ask him his age.

YOUNG MARTIN. My lord, (*hesitantly*) how old are him? I mean 'you' . . .

ATAHUALLPA. I have been on earth thirty and three years. What age is your master?

YOUNG MARTIN. Sixty-three.

ATAHUALLPA. All those years have taught him nothing but wickedness.

YOUNG MARTIN. That's not true.

PIZARRO. What does he say?

YOUNG MARTIN. I don't quite understand, my lord . . .

    Exit YOUNG MARTIN.

OLD MARTIN. So it was I became the General's interpreter and was privy to everything that passed between them during the next months. The Inca tongue was very hard, but to please my adored master I worked at it for hours, and with each passing day found out more of it.

    PIZARRO *leaves, followed by* DE SOTO.

Act Two – The Kill

III

Re-enter YOUNG MARTIN *above.* OLD MARTIN *watches below before going off.*

YOUNG MARTIN. Good day, my lord. I have a game here to amuse you. No Spaniard is complete without them. I take half and you take half. Then we fight. These are the Churchmen with their pyxes. The Nobility with their swords. The Merchants with their gold, and the Poor with their sticks.

ATAHUALLPA. What are the poor?

YOUNG MARTIN. Those who've got no gold. They suffer for this.

ATAHUALLPA (*crying out*). Aiyah!

YOUNG MARTIN. What are you thinking, my lord?

ATAHUALLPA. That my people will suffer.

Enter PIZARRO *and* DE SOTO.

PIZARRO. Good day, my lord. How are you this morning?

ATAHUALLPA. You want gold. That is why you came here.

PIZARRO. My lord—

ATAHUALLPA. You can't hide from me. (*Showing him the card of the Poor*) You want gold. I know. Speak.

PIZARRO. You have gold?

ATAHUALLPA. It is the sweat of the sun. It belongs to me.

PIZARRO. Is there much?

ATAHUALLPA. Make me free. I would fill this room.

PIZARRO. Fill?

DE SOTO. It's not possible.

ATAHUALLPA. I am Atahuallpa and I say it.

PIZARRO. How long?

ATAHUALLPA. Two showings of my Mother Moon. But it will not be done.

PIZARRO. Why not?

ATAHUALLPA. You must swear to free me and you have no swear to give.

PIZARRO. You wrong me, my lord.

E   43

ATAHUALLPA. No, it is in your face, no swear.

PIZARRO. I never broke word with you. I never promised you safety. If once I did, you would have it.

ATAHUALLPA. Do you now?

DE SOTO. Refuse, sir. You could never free him.

PIZARRO. It won't come to that.

DE SOTO. It could.

PIZARRO. Never. Can you think how much gold it would take? Even half would drown us in riches.

DE SOTO. General, you can only give your word where you can keep it.

PIZARRO. I'll never have to break it. It's the same case.

DE SOTO. It's not.

PIZARRO. Oh, God's wounds, your niceties! He's offering more than any conqueror has even seen. Alexander, Tamberlaine, or who you please. I mean to have it.

DE SOTO. So. At your age gold is no lodestone!

PIZARRO. No more is it. I promised my men gold. Yes? He stands between them and that gold. If I don't make this bargain now he'll die; the men will demand it.

DE SOTO. And what's that to you if he does?

PIZARRO. I want him alive. At least for a while.

DE SOTO. You're thinking of how you dreamed of him.

PIZARRO. Yes. He has some meaning for me, this Man-God. An immortal man in whom all his people live completely. He has an answer for time.

DE SOTO. If it was true.

PIZARRO. Yes, if . . .

DE SOTO. General, be careful. I don't understand you in full but I know this: what you do now can never be undone.

PIZARRO. Words, my dear Cavalier. They don't touch me. This way I'll have gold for my men and him there safe. That's enough for the moment. (*To* ATAHUALLPA) Now you must keep the peace meanwhile, not strive to escape, nor urge your men to help you. So swear.

ATAHUALLPA. I swear!

PIZARRO. Then I swear too. Fill that room with gold and I will set you free.

DE SOTO. General!

PIZARRO. Oh, come man! He never will.

DE SOTO. I think this man performs what he swears. Pray God we don't pay bitterly for this.

He goes off. Enter OLD MARTIN.

PIZARRO. My lord – (ATAHUALLPA *ignores him*) – well spoken, lad. Your services increase every day.

YOUNG MARTIN. Thank you, sir.

The General leaves the stage and the boy goes out of the Sun chamber, leaving ATAHUALLPA *alone in it.*

OLD MARTIN. The room was twenty-two feet long by seventeen feet wide. The mark on the wall was nine feet high.

The Inca adopts a pose of command. Drums mark each name.

ATAHUALLPA. Atahuallpa speaks! (*A crash of instruments*) Atahuallpa needs. (*Crash*) Atahuallpa commands. (*Crash*) Bring him gold. From the palaces. From the temples. From all buildings in the great places. From walls of pleasure and roofs of omen. From floors of feasting and ceilings of death. Bring him the gold of Quito and Pachamacac! Bring him the gold of Cuzco and Coricancha! Bring him the gold of Vilcanota! Bring him the gold of Colae! Of Aymaraes and Arequipa! Bring him the gold of the Chimu! Put up a mountain of gold and free your Sun from his prison of clouds.

Lights down above. ATAHUALLPA *leaves the chamber.*

OLD MARTIN. It was agreed that the gold collected was not to be melted beforehand into bars, so that the Inca got the benefit of the space between them. Then he was moved out of his prison to make way for the treasure and given more comfortable state.

45

IV

Lights fade above, and brighten below.

Slowly the great cloth of blood is dragged off by two Indians as ATAHUALLPA *appears. He advances to the middle of the stage. He claps his hands, once. Immediately a gentle hum is heard and Indians appear with new clothing. From their wrists hang tiny golden cymbals and small bells; to the soft clash and tinkle of these little instruments his servant removes the Inca's bloodstained garments and puts on him clean ones.*

OLD MARTIN. He was allowed to audience his nobles. The little loads they bore were a sign of reverence.

    VILLAC UMU *and* CHALLCUCHIMA *come in.*

He was dressed in his royal cloak, made from the skins of vampire birds, and his ears were hung again with the weight of noble responsibility.

    ATAHUALLPA *is cloaked, a collar of turquoises is placed round his neck and heavy gold rings are placed in his ears. While this is happening there is a fresh tinkling and more Indians appear, carrying his meal in musical dishes – plates like tambourines from whose rims hang bells, or in whose lower shelves are tiny golden balls. The stage is filled with chimes and delicate clatter, and above it the perpetual humming of masked servants.*

OLD MARTIN. His meals are served as they always had been. I remember his favourite food was stewed lamb, garnished with sweet potatoes.

    The food is served to the Inca in this manner. OELLO *takes meat out of a bowl, places it in her hands and* ATAHUALLPA *lowers his face to it, while she turns her own face away from him out of respect.*

OLD MARTIN. What he didn't eat was burnt, and if he spilled any on himself, his clothes were burnt also. (*Exit*)

    OELLO *rises and quietly removes the dish. Suddenly*

FELIPILLO *rushes on and knocks it violently from her hand.*

FELIPILLO. You're going to burn it? Why? Because your husband is a God? How stupid! stupid! stupid!

He grabs her and flings her to the ground. A general cry of horror.

(*To* ATAHUALLPA) Yes, I touch her! Make me dead! You are a God. Make me dead with your eyes!

VILLAC UMU. What you have said kills you. You will be buried in the earth alive.

A pause. For a moment FELIPILLO *half believes this. Then he laughs and kisses the girl on the throat. As she screams and struggles,* YOUNG MARTIN *rushes in.*

YOUNG MARTIN. Felipillo, stop it!

VALVERDE *comes in from another side, with* DE NIZZA.

VALVERDE. Felipillo! Is it for this we saved you from Hell? Your old God encouraged lust. Your new God will damn you for it. Leave him!

FELIPILLO *runs off.*

(*To the* INDIANS) Go!

A pause. No one moves until ATAHUALLPA *claps his hands twice. Then all the servants bow and leave.*

Now, my lord, let us take up our talk again. Tell me – I am only a simple priest – as an undoubted God, do you live forever here on earth?

VILLAC UMU. Here on earth Gods come one after another, young and young again, to protect the people of the Sun. Then they go up to his great place in the sky, at his will.

VALVERDE. What if they are killed in battle?

VILLAC UMU. If it is not the Sun's time for them to go, he will return them to life again in the next day's light.

VALVERDE. How comforting. And has any Inca so returned?

VILLAC UMU. No.

VALVERDE. Curious.

47

VILLAC UMU. This means only that all Incas have died in the Sun's time.

VALVERDE. Clever.

VILAC UMU. No. True.

VALVERDE. Tell me this, how can the Sun have a child?

VILLAC UMU. How can your God have a Child, since you say he has no body?

VALVERDE. He is a spirit – inside us.

VILLAC UMU. Your God is inside you? How can this be?

ATAHUALLPA. They eat him. First he becomes a biscuit, and then they eat him. (*The Inca bares his teeth and laughs soundlessly*) I have seen this. At praying they say 'This is the body of our God'. Then they drink his blood. It is very bad. Here in my empire we do not eat men. My family forbade it many years past.

VALVERDE. You are being deliberately stupid.

VILLAC UMU. Why do you eat your God? To have his strength?

DE NIZZA. Yes, my lord.

VILLAC UMU. But your God is weak. He fights with no man. That is why he was killed.

DE NIZZA. He wanted to be killed, so he could share death with us.

ATAHUALLPA. So he needed killers to help him, though you say killing is bad.

VALVERDE. This is the devil's tongue.

DE NIZZA. My lord must see that when God becomes man, he can no longer act perfectly.

ATAHUALLPA. Why?

DE NIZZA. He joins us in our state of sin.

ATAHUALLPA. What is sin?

DE NIZZA. Let me picture it to you as a prison cell, the bars made of our imperfections. Through them we glimpse a fair country where it is always morning. We wish we could walk there, or else forget the place entirely. But we cannot snap the bars, or if we do, others grow in their stead.

ATAHUALLPA. All your pictures are of prisons and chains.

DE NIZZA. All life is chains. We are chained to food, and

fire in the winter. To innocence lost but its memory unlost.
And to needing each other.

ATAHUALLPA. I need no one.

DE NIZZA. That is not true.

ATAHUALLPA. I am the Sun. I need only the sky.

DE NIZZA. That is not true, Atahuallpa. The sun is a ball of
fire. Nothing more.

ATAHUALLPA. How?

DE NIZZA. Nothing more.

> *With terrible speed, the* INCA *rises to strike* DE
> NIZZA.

VALVERDE. Down! Do you dare lift your hand against a
priest? Sit! Now!

> ATAHUALLPA *does not move.*

DE NIZZA. You do not feel your people, my lord, because
you do not love them.

ATAHUALLPA. Explain love.

DE NIZZA. It is not known in your kingdom. At home we
can say to our ladies: 'I love you', or to our native earth. It
means we rejoice in their lives. But a man cannot say this
to the woman he must marry at twenty-five; or to the strip
of land allotted to him at birth which he must till until he
dies. Love must be free, or else it alters away. Command
it to your court: it will send a deputy. Let God order it to
fill our hearts, it becomes useless to him. It is stronger than
iron: yet in a fist or force it melts. It is a coin that sparkles
in the hand: yet in the pocket it turns to rust. Love is the
only door from the prison of ourselves. It is the eagerness
of God to enter that prison, to take on pain, and imagine
lust, so that the torn soldier, or the spent lecher, can call
out in his defeat: 'You know this too, so help me from it.'

> *A further music of bells and humming. Enter* OLD
> MARTIN.

THE FIRST GOLD PROCESSION

> *Guarded closely by Spanish soldiers, a line of Indian
> porters comes in, each carrying a stylized gold object*

The Royal Hunt of the Sun

– utensils and ornaments. They cross the stage and disappear. Almost simultaneously, above, similar objects are hung up by Indians in the middle of the sun.

OLD MARTIN (*during this*). The first gold arrived. Much of it was in big plates weighing up to seventy-five pounds, the rest in objects of amazing skill. Knives of ceremony; collars and fretted crowns; funeral gloves, and red-stained death masks, goggling at us with profound enamel eyes. Some days there were things worth thirty or forty gold pesos – but we weren't satisfied with that. (*Exit*).

Enter PIZARRO *and* DE SOTO.

PIZARRO. I find you wanting in honesty. A month has passed: the room isn't a quarter full.

ATAHUALLPA. My kingdom is great; porters are slow. You will see more gold before long.

PIZARRO. The rumour is we'll see a rising before long.

ATAHUALLPA. Not a leaf stirs in my kingdom without my leave. If you do not trust me send to Cuzco, my capital. See how quiet my people sit.

PIZARRO (*to* DE SOTO). Good. You leave immediately with a force of thirty.

CHALCUCHIMA. God is tied by his word, like you. But if he raise one nail of one finger of one hand, you would all die that same raising.

PIZARRO. So be it. If you play us false, both these will die before us.

ATAHUALLPA. There are many Priests, many Generals. These can die.

VALVERDE. Mother of God! There's no conversion possible for this man.

DE SOTO. You cannot say that, sir.

VALVERDE. Satan has many forms and there sits one. As for his advisers, it is you, Priest, who stiffen him against me. You, General, who whisper revolt.

CHALCUCHIMA. You lie.

VALVERDE. Leave him!

As before they do not move until ATAHUALLPA

50

has clapped his hands twice. Then, immediately,
the two Indians bow and leave.

Pagan filth.

DE SOTO. I'll make inspection. Good-bye my lord, we'll meet
in a month.

Exit DE SOTO.

VALVERDE. Beware Pizarro. Give him the slack, he will
destroy us all.

He goes out another way.

DE NIZZA. The Father has great zeal.

PIZARRO. Oh, yes, great zeal to see the devil in a poor dark
man.

DE NIZZA. Not so poor, General. A man who is the soul of
his kingdom. Look hard, you *will* find Satan here, because
here is a country which denies the right to hunger.

PIZARRO. You call hunger a right?

DE NIZZA. Of course, it gives life meaning. Look around
you: happiness has no feel for men here since they are
forbidden unhappiness. They have everything in common
so they have nothing to give each other. They are part of
the seasons, no more; as indistinguishable as mules, as
predictable as trees. All men are born unequal: this is a
divine gift. And want is their birthright. Where you deny
this and there is no hope of any new love; where tomorrow is abolished, and no man ever thinks 'I can change
myself', there you have the rule of Anti-Christ. Atahuallpa, I will not rest until I have brought you to the
true God.

ATAHUALLPA. No! He is not true! Where is he? There is
my father-Sun! You see now only by his wish; yet try to
see into him and he will darken your eyes for ever. With
hot burning he pulls the corn and we feed. With cold
burning he shrinks it and we starve. These are his burn-
ings and our life. Do not speak to me again of your God:
he is nowhere.

PIZARRO *laughs. Hurriedly* DE NIZZA *leaves.*

V

PIZARRO. You said you'd hear the Holy Men.
ATAHUALLPA. They are fools.
PIZARRO. They are not fools.
ATAHUALLPA. Do you believe them?
PIZARRO. For certain.
ATAHUALLPA. Look into me.
PIZARRO. Your eyes are smoking wood.
ATAHUALLPA. You do not believe them.
PIZARRO. You dare not say that to me . . .
ATAHUALLPA. You do not believe them. Their God is not in
your face.

> PIZARRO *retreats from* ATAHUALLPA, *who be-*
> *gins to sing in a strange voice:*

> You must not rob, O little finch.
> The harvest maize, O little finch.
> The trap is set, O little finch.
> To seize you quick, O little finch.

> Ask that black bird, O little finch.
> Nailed on a branch, O little finch.
> Where is her heart, O little finch.
> Where are her plumes, O little finch.

> She is cut up, O little finch.
> For stealing grain, O little finch.
> See, see the fate, O little finch.
> Of robber birds, O little finch.

This is a harvest song. For you.
PIZARRO. For me?
ATAHUALLPA. Yes.
PIZARRO. Robber birds.
ATAHUALLPA. Yes.
PIZARRO. You're a robber bird yourself.

ATAHUALLPA. Explain this.

PIZARRO. You killed your brother to get the throne.

ATAHUALLPA. He was a fool. His body was a man. His head was a child.

PIZARRO. But he was the rightful king.

ATAHUALLPA. I was the rightful God. My Sky Father shouted 'Rise up! In you lives your Earth Father, Huayana the Warrior. Your brother is fit only to tend herds but you were born to tend my people.' So I killed him, and the land smiled.

PIZARRO. That was my work long ago. Tending herds.

ATAHUALLPA. It was not your work. You are a warrior. It is in your face.

PIZARRO. You see much in my face.

ATAHUALLPA. I see your father.

PIZARRO. You do me honour, lad.

ATAHUALLPA. Speak true. If in your home your brother was King, but fit only for herds, would you take his crown?

PIZARRO. If I could.

ATAHUALLPA. And then you would kill him.

PIZARRO. No.

ATAHUALLPA. If you could not keep it for fear of his friends, unless he was dead, you would kill him.

PIZARRO. Let me give you another case. If I come to a country and seize the King's crown, but for fear of his friends cannot keep it unless I kill him, what do I do?

ATAHUALLPA. So.

PIZARRO. So.

    ATAHUALLPA *moves away, offended.*

Oh, it is only a game we play. Tell me – did you hate your brother?

ATAHUALLPA. No. He was ugly like a llama, like his mother. My mother was beautiful.

PIZARRO. I did not know my mother. She was not my father's wife. She left me at the church door for anyone to find. There's talk in the village still, how I was suckled by a sow.

ATAHUALLPA. You are not then . . . ?

PIZARRO. Legitimate? No, my lord, no more than you.

ATAHUALLPA. So.

PIZARRO. So.

A pause.

ATAHUALLPA. To be born so is a sign for a great man.

PIZARRO (*smiling*). I think so too.

> ATAHUALLPA *removes one of his golden earrings and hangs it on* PIZARRO'S *ear.*

And what is that?

ATAHUALLPA. The sign of a nobleman. Only the most important men may wear them, The most near to me.

YOUNG MARTIN. Very becoming, sir. Look.

> *He hands him a dagger. The General looks at himself in the blade.*

PIZARRO. I have never seemed so distinguished to myself. I thank you.

ATAHUALLPA. Now you must learn the dance of the aylu.

YOUNG MARTIN. The dance of a nobleman, sir.

ATAHUALLPA. Only he can do this. I will show you.

> PIZARRO *sits.* ATAHUALLPA *dances a ferocious mime of a warrior killing his foes. It is very difficult to execute, demanding great litheness and physical stamina. As suddenly as it began, it is over.*

ATAHUALLPA. You dance.

PIZARRO. I can't dance, lad.

ATAHUALLPA (*sternly*). You dance.

> *He sits to watch. Seeing there is no help for it,* PIZARRO *rises and clumsily tries to copy the dance. The effect is so grotesque that* YOUNG MARTIN *cannot help laughing. The General tries again, lunges, slips, slides, and finally starts to laugh himself. He gives up the attempt.*

PIZARRO (*to* ATAHUALLPA). You make me laugh! (*In sudden wonder.*) *You make me laugh!*

> ATAHUALLPA *consults his young interpreter, who tries to explain. The Inca nods gravely. Tentatively* PIZARRO *extends his hand to him.* ATAHUALLPA *takes it and rises. Quietly they go off together.*

Act Two – The Kill

VI

Enter OLD MARTIN.

OLD MARTIN. Slowly the pile increased. The army waited nervously and licked its lips. Greed began to rise in us like a tide of sea.
A music of bells and humming.

THE SECOND GOLD PROCESSION
and THE RAPE OF THE SUN.

Another line of Indian porters comes in, bearing gold objects. Like the first, this instalment of treasure is guarded by Spanish soldiers, but they are less disciplined now. Two of them assault an Indian and grab his headdress. Another snatches a necklace at sword's point.

Above, in the chamber, the treasure is piled up as before. DIEGO *and the* CHAVEZ *brothers are seen supervising. They begin to explore the sun itself, leaning out of the chamber and prodding at the petals with their halberds. Suddenly* DIEGO *gives a cry of triumph, drives his halberd into a slot in one of the rays, and pulls out the gold inlay. The sun gives a deep groan, like the sound of a great animal being wounded. With greedy yelps, all the soldiers below rush at the sun and start pulling it to bits; they tear out the gold inlays and fling them on the ground, while terrible groans fill the air. In a moment only the great gold frame remains; a broken, blackened sun.*

Enter DE SOTO.

DIEGO. Welcome back, sir.

DE SOTO. Diego, it's good to see you.

DIEGO. What's it like, sir? Is there trouble?

DE SOTO. It's grave quiet. Terrible. Men just standing in

55

fields for hundreds of miles. Waiting for their God to come back to them.

DIEGO. Well, if he does they'll be fighters again and we're for the limepit.

DE SOTO. How's the General?

DIEGO. An altered man. No one's ever seen him so easy. He spends hours each day with the King. He's going to find it hard when he has to do it.

DE SOTO. Do what?

DIEGO. Kill him, sir.

DE SOTO. He can't do that. Not after a contract witnessed before a whole army.

DIEGO. Well, he can't let him go, that's for certain . . . Never mind, he'll find a way. He's as cunning as the devil's gran-dad, save your pardon, sir.

DE SOTO. No, you're right, boy.

DIEGO. Tell us about their capital, then. What's it like?

During the preceding, a line of Indians, bent double, has been loaded with the torn-off petals from the sun. Now, as DE SOTO *describes Cuzco, they file slowly round the stage and go off, staggering under the weight of the great gold slabs. When he reaches the account of the garden, the marvellous objects he tells of appear in the treasure chamber above, borne by Indians, and are stacked up until they fill it com-pletely. The interior of the sun is now a solid mass of gold.*

DE SOTO. Completely round. They call it the navel of the earth and that's what it looks like. In the middle was a huge temple, the centre of their faith. The walls were plated with gold, enough to blind us. Inside, set out on tables, golden platters for the sun to dine off. Outside, the garden: acres of gold soil planted with gold maize. Entire apple trees in gold. Gold birds on the branches. Gold geese and ducks. Gold butterflies in the air on silver strings. And – imagine this – away in a field, life-size, twenty golden llamas grazing with their kids. The garden of the Sun at Cuzco. A wonder of the earth. Look at it now.

DIEGO (*rushing in below*). Hey! The room's full!

DOMINGO. It isn't!

SALINAS. It is. Look!

JUAN. He's right. It's full!

DIEGO. We can start the share-out now. (*Cheers*)

PEDRO. What'll you do with your lot, Juan, boy?

JUAN. Buy a farm.

PEDRO. Me, too. I don't work for nobody ever again.

DOMINGO. Ah, you can buy a palace, easy, with a share of that. Never mind a pissing farm! What d'you say, Diego?

DIEGO. Oh, I want a farm, A good stud farm, and a stable of Arabs, just for me to ride! What will you have, Salinas?

SALINAS. Me? A bash-house! (*Laughter*) Right in the middle of Trujillo, open six to six, filled with saddle-backed fillies from Andalusia ...

Enter VASCA *rolling a huge gold sun, like a hoop.*

VASCA. Look what I got, boys! The sun! He ain't public any more, the old sun. He's private property!

DOMINGO. There's no private property, till share out.

VASCA. Well, here's the exception. I risked my life to get this a hundred feet up.

JUAN. Dungballs!

VASCA. I did! Off the temple roof.

PEDRO. Come on, boy, get it up there with the rest.

VASCA. No. Finding's keepings. That's the law.

JUAN. What law?

VASCA. My law. Do you think you'll see any of this once the share-out starts? Not on your pissing life. You leave it up there, boy, you won't see nothing again.

PEDRO (*to his brother*). He's right there.

JUAN. Do you think so?

VASCA. Of course. Officers first, then the Church. You'll get pissing nothing. (*A pause*)

SALINAS. So let's have a share-out now, then!

DOMINGO. Why not? We're all entitled.

VASCA. Of course we are.

JUAN. All right. I'm with you.

PEDRO. Good boy!

SALINAS. Come on, then.

They all make a rush for the Sun Chamber.

DE SOTO. Where do you think you're going? . . . You know the General's orders. Nothing till share-out. Penalty for breach, death. Disperse now. I'll go and see the General.

They hesitate.

(*Quietly*) Get to your posts.

Reluctantly, they disperse.

And keep a sharp watch. The danger's not over yet.

DIEGO. I'd say it had only just begun, sir.

He goes. DE SOTO *remains.*

VII

Enter PIZARRO *and* ATAHUALLPA *duelling furiously;* YOUNG MARTIN *behind. The Inca is a magnificent fighter and launches himself vigorously on the old man, finally knocking the sword from his hand.*

PIZARRO. Enough! You exhaust me . . .

ATAHUALLPA. I fight well – 'ye-es'?

From the difficulty he has with this word, it is evident that it is in Spanish.

PIZARRO (*imitating him*). 'Ye-es'! . . . Like a hidalgo!

YOUNG MARTIN. Magnificent, my lord.

PIZARRO. I'm proud of you.

ATAHUALLPA. Chica!

YOUNG MARTIN. Maize wine, sir.

PIZARRO. De Soto! – A drink, my dear second.

DE SOTO. With pleasure, General, the room is full.

PIZARRO (*casually*). I know it.

DE SOTO. My advice to you is to share out right away. The men are just on the turn.

PIZARRO. I think so too.

DE SOTO. We daren't delay.

PIZARRO. Agreed. Now I shall astound you, Cavalier. Atahuallpa, you have learnt how a Spaniard fights. Now you will learn his honour. Martin, your pen. (*Dictating*) 'Let this be known throughout my army. The Inca Atahuallpa has today discharged his obligation to General Pizarro. He is therefore a free man.'

DE SOTO (*toasting him*). My lord, your freedom!

> ATAHUALLPA *kneels. Silently he mouths words of gratitude to the sun.*

ATAHUALLPA. Atahuallpa thanks the lord de Soto, the lord Pizarro, all lords of honour. You may touch my joy.

> *He extends his arms. Both Spaniards help to raise him.*

DE SOTO. What happens now?

PIZARRO. I release him. He must swear first, of course, not to harm us.

DE SOTO. Do you think he will?

PIZARRO. For me he will.

ATAHUALLPA (*to the boy*). What is that you have done?

YOUNG MARTIN. Writing, my lord.

ATAHUALLPA. Explain this.

YOUNG MARTIN. These are signs: This is 'Atahuallpa', and this is 'ransom'.

ATAHUALLPA. You put this sign, and he will see and know 'ransom'?

YOUNG MARTIN. Yes.

ATAHUALLPA. No.

YOUNG MARTIN. Yes, my lord. I'll do it again.

ATAHUALLPA. Here, on my nail. Do not say what you put.

> YOUNG MARTIN *writes on his nail.*

YOUNG MARTIN. Now show it to Cavalier de Soto.

> *He does so.* DE SOTO *reads and whispers the word to* ATAHUALLPA.

ATAHUALLPA (*to the boy*). What is put?

YOUNG MARTIN. God.

ATAHUALLPA (*amazed*). God! . . . (*He stares at his nail in fascination then bursts into delighted laughter, like a child.*) Show me again! Another sign!

The boy writes on another nail.

PIZARRO. Tell Salinas to take five hundred Indians and melt everything down.

DE SOTO. Everything?

PIZARRO. We can't transport it as it is.

DE SOTO. But there are objects of great beauty, sir. In all my service I've never seen treasure like this. Work subtler than anything in Italy.

PIZARRO. You're a tender man.

ATAHUALLPA (*extending his nail to* PIZARRO). What is put?

PIZARRO (*who of course cannot read*). Put?

ATAHUALLPA. Here.

PIZARRO. This is a foolish game.

YOUNG MARTIN. The General never learnt the skill, my lord. (*An embarrassed pause*) A soldier does not need it.
ATAHUALLPA *stares at him.*

ATAHUALLPA. A King needs it. There is great power in these marks. You are the King in this room. You must teach us two. We will learn together – like brothers.

PIZARRO. You would stay with me here, to learn?
Pause.

ATAHUALLPA. No. Tomorrow I will go.

PIZARRO. And then? What will you do then?

ATAHUALLPA. I will not hurt you.

PIZARRO. Or my army?

ATAHUALLPA. That I do not swear.

PIZARRO. You must.

ATAHUALLPA. You do not say this till now.

PIZARRO. Well, now I say it. Atahuallpa, you must swear to me that you will not hurt a man in my army if I let you go.

ATAHUALLPA. I will not swear this.

PIZARRO. For my sake.

ATAHUALLPA. Three thousand of my servants they killed in the square. Three thousand, without arms. I will avenge them.

PIZARRO. There is a way of mercy, Atahuallpa.

ATAHUALLPA. It is not my way. It is not your way.

PIZARRO. Well, show it to me, then.

ATAHUALLPA. Keep your swear first.

PIZARRO. That I cannot do.

ATAHUALLPA. Cannot?

PIZARRO. Not immediately . . . you must see: you are many, we are few.

ATAHUALLPA. This is not important.

PIZARRO. To me it is.

> ATAHUALLPA *hisses with fury. He strides across the room and before* PIZARRO'S *face makes a violent gesture with his hand between their two mouths.*

ATAHUALLPA (*violently*). You gave a word!

PIZARRO. And will keep it. Only not now. Not today.

ATAHUALLPA. When?

PIZARRO. Soon.

ATAHUALLPA. When?

PIZARRO. Very soon.

ATAHUALLPA (*falling on his knees and beating the ground*). *When?*

PIZARRO. As soon as you promise not to hurt my army.

ATAHUALLPA (*with wild rage*). I will kill every man of them! I will make drums of their bodies! I will beat music on them at my great feasts!

PIZARRO (*provoked*). Boy – what have I put?

YOUNG MARTIN. 'He is therefore a free man.'

PIZARRO. Continue: 'But for the welfare of the country, he will remain for the moment as guest of the army.'

DE SOTO. What does that mean?

ATAHUALLPA. What does he say?

PIZARRO. Don't translate.

DE SOTO. So it's started. My warning was nothing to you.

PIZARRO. Well, gloat, gloat!

DE SOTO. I don't gloat.

ATAHUALLPA. What does he say?

PIZARRO. Nothing.

ATAHUALLPA. There is fear in his face!

PIZARRO. *Be quiet!* . . . (*To* DE SOTO) I want all the gold in blocks. Leave nothing unmelted. Attend to it yourself, personally!

61

DE SOTO *goes abruptly.* OLD MARTIN *appears in the background.* PIZARRO *is trembling.*

PIZARRO (*to the page*). Well, what are you staring at, Little Lord Chivalry? Get out!

YOUNG MARTIN. He trusts you, sir.

PIZARRO. Trust: what's that? Another word. Honour . . . glory . . . trust: your word – Gods!

YOUNG MARTIN. You can see it, sir. He trusts you.

PIZARRO. I told you: out.

YOUNG MARTIN (*greatly daring*). You can't betray him, sir. You can't.

PIZARRO. Damn you – impertinence!

YOUNG MARTIN. I don't care, sir. You just can't! (*He stops*)

PIZARRO. In all your study of those admirable writers, you never learned the duty a page owes his master. I am sorry you have not better fulfilled your first office. There will be no other.

The boy makes to go out.

A salute, if you please.

He bows.

Time was when we couldn't stop you.

YOUNG MARTIN *leaves.* PIZARRO *stares after him, shaking.*

OLD MARTIN. I went out into the night – the cold high night of the Andes, hung with stars like crystal apples – and dropped my first tears as a man. My first and last. That was my first and last worship too. Devotion never came again. (*Exit*)

With a moan, PIZARRO *collapses on the floor and lies writhing in pain.* ATAHUALLPA *contemplates his captor with surprised disdain. But slowly, as the old man's agony continues, contempt in the King is replaced by a gentler emotion. Curious, he kneels. Uncertain what to do, he extends his hands, first to the wound, and then to* PIZARRO'S *head, which he holds with a kind of remote tenderness. The lights go down all around them.*

PIZARRO. Leave it now. There's no cure or more easing for

it. Death's entered the house you see. It's half down already, like an old barn. What can you know about that? Youth's in you like a spring of blood, to spurt for ever. Your skin is singing: 'I will never get old.' But you will. Time is stalking you, as I did. That gold flesh will cold and blacken. Your eyes will curdle, those wet living eyes . . . They'll make a mummy of your body – I know the custom – and wrap you in robes of vicuna wool, and carry you through all your Empire down to Cuzco. And then they'll fold you in two and sit you on a chair in darkness . . . Atahuallpa, I'm going to die! And the thought of that dark has for years rotted everything for me, all simple joy in life. All through old age, which is so much longer and more terrible than anything in youth, I've watched the circles of nature with hatred. The leaves pop out, the leaves fall. Every year it's piglet time, calving time, time for children in a gush of blood and water. Women dote on this. A birth, any birth, fills them with love. They clap with love, and my soul shrugs. Round and round is all I see: an endless sky of birds, flying and ripping and nursing their young to fly and rip and nurse their young – for what? Listen, boy. That prison the Priest calls Sin Original, I know as Time. And seen in time everything is trivial. Pain. Good. God is trivial in that seeing. Trapped in this cage we cry out 'There's a gaoler; there must be. At the last, last, last of lasts he will let us out. He will! He will!' . . . But, oh my boy, no one will come out for all our crying. (*Pause*) I'm going to kill you, Atahuallpa. What does it matter? Words kept, words broken, it all means nothing. Nothing. You go to sleep earlier than me, that's all. Do you see? Look at your eyes, like coals from the sun, glowing forever in the deep of your skull. Like my dream . . . Sing me your little song. (*Singing.*) O little finch. . . .

ATAHUALLPA *intones a few lines of the song.*
Nothing. Nothing . . . (*In sudden anguish, almost hatred*) O, lad, what am I going to do with you?

VIII

A red light up above.

OLD MARTIN *appears above in the Sun Chamber. Violent music, the sound of destruction. The light fades and comes up on stage where the soldiers assemble.*

OLD MARTIN. Nine forges were kept alight for three weeks. The masterwork of centuries was banged down into fat bars, four hundred and forty pounds each day. The booty exceeded all other known in history: the sack of Genoa, Milan or even Rome. Share-out started at once. (*Exit*)

DIEGO. General Francisco Pizarro, 57,220 gold pesos. Hernando de Soto, 17,740 gold pesos. The Holy Church, 2,220 gold pesos.

    Enter ESTETE *and* DE CANDIA.

ESTETE. And a fifth of everything, of course, to the Crown.

PIZARRO. You come in good time, Veedor.

ESTETE. So it seems! Cavalier.

DE SOTO. Veedor.

PIZARRO. Welcome, de Candia.

DE CANDIA. Thank you. (*Indicating the ear-ring*) I see the living's become soft here already. The men hung with jewels like fops at Court.

PIZARRO. You set the fashion: I only follow.

DE CANDIA. I'm flattered.

PIZARRO. What news of the reinforcements?

DE CANDIA. None.

ESTETE. I sent runners back to the coast. They saw nothing.

PIZARRO. So we're cut off, here. How's my garrison?

DE CANDIA. Spanish justice reigns supreme. They hang Indians for everything. How's your royal friend? When do we hang him?

    Pause. PIZARRO *tears off his ear-ring and flings it on the floor.*

PIZARRO. Finish the share-out.

    Violently he leaves them. The men stare after him.

DE SOTO. Go on Diego. Tell us the rest . . . *Go on,* man!

DIEGO. The remainder – cavalry, infantry, clerks, farriers, coopers and the like – will divide a total of 971,000 gold pesos!

Cheers. Enter RODAS.

SALINAS. Well, look. Our little tailor! How are you, friend?

RODAS. Hungry. What do I get?

SALINAS. A kick up the tunnel.

RODAS. Ho, ha. Day of a hundred jokes! I got a right to a share.

DOMINGO. What for?

RODAS. I stayed behind and guarded your pissing rear, that's what for.

DE SOTO. You've no right, Rodas. As far as you cared we could all rot, remember? Well, now you get nothing; the proper wage for cowardice.

General agreement. The men settle upstage to a game of dice.

(*To* ESTETE) I must wait on the General.

ESTETE. I am sorry to see him still subject to distresses. I had hoped that victory would have brought him calmer temper.

DE CANDIA. It must be his new wealth, Veedor. So much, so sudden, must be a great burden to him.

DE SOTO. The burdens of the General, sir, are care for his men, and for our present situation. Let us try to lighten them for him as we can.

He goes off.

DE CANDIA. Let us indeed. One throat cut and we're all lightened.

ESTETE. It would much relieve the Crown if you'd cut it.

DE CANDIA. If I . . . ? You mean I'm not Spanish, I don't have to trouble with honour.

ESTETE. You're not a subject. It could be disowned by my King. And you have none.

DE CANDIA. So the Palace of Disinterest has a shit-house after all. Look man, you're the overseer here, so do your job. Go to the General and tell him the brownie must go.

65

And add this from me: if Spain waits any longer, Venice will act for herself.

They go off. Enter OLD MARTIN.

IX

A scene of tension and growing violence. The soldiers, now dirty almost beyond recognition, but wearing ornaments, earrings and headdresses stolen from the treasure, dice for gold. They are watched silently from above by a line of masked Indians carrying instruments for making bird noises. A drum begins to beat. PIZARRO *stumbles in, and during the whole ensuing scene limps to and fro across the stage like a caged animal, ignoring everything but his own mental pain.*

OLD MARTIN. Morale began to go fast. Day after day we watched his private struggle, and the brownies watched us, waiting one sign from the frozen boy to get up and kill the lot of us.

DOMINGO. Play up, then!

PEDRO. Two fours.

JUAN throws successfully.

JUAN (*grabbing a gold bar belonging to* PEDRO). That's mine, boy.

PEDRO. No – Juan!

JUAN. Give it. (*He snatches it*)

DOMINGO. They say there's an army gathering in the mountains. At least five thousand of them.

VASCA. I heard that too.

DOMINGO. Blas says there's some of them cannibals.

Bird cries.

SALINAS. That's just stories. Pissing stupid stories. You don't want to listen to 'em.

RODAS. I'd like to see you when they tie you to the spit.

VASCA (*rolling the dice*). Turn up! Turn up! Turn up!

RODAS. Come on boys, cut me in.

VASCA. Piss off! No stake, no play.

RODAS. Bloody bastards!

DOMINGO. They say it's led by the Inca's top general. The brownies are full of his name.

VASCA. What is it? Rumi . . . Rumi . . . ?

DOMINGO. That's it. Ruminagui, something like that.

The Indians above repeat the name in a low menacing chant: RU-MIN-Ā-GUI! *The soldiers look fearfully about them. The bird cries sound again.*

SALINAS. Come on, then, let's play.

VASCA. What for? The sun?

SALINAS. The sun!

VASCA. Turn up! Turn up! Turn up! Turn up! King and ten. Beat that!

SALINAS. Holy Mary, mother of Christ. Save my soul and bless my dice. (*He throws*) Two Kings . . . I did it! I'm sorry, lads, but that's your sun gone.

VASCA. Go on, then. Let's see you pick it up.

SALINAS bends and tries to shift it. VASCA *laughs. The bird cries grow wilder.*

RODAS. He can't even lift it, but I can't play!

SALINAS. I'll settle for these.

He picks up three gold bars and walks off with them.

RODAS *trips him up and he goes sprawling.*

Christ damn you, Rodas – that's the pissing last I take from you.

He springs at RODAS and clouts him with a gold bar. The tailor howls, picks up another, and a fight starts between them which soon becomes a violent free-for-all. The men shout; the birds scream; the General paces to and fro, ignoring everything. Finally DE SOTO rushes on just in time as SALINAS tries to strangle RODAS. He is followed by ESTETE and the two priests, who attend to the wounded.

DE SOTO. *Stop this!* . . . Do you want to start it all off?

Silence. All the Indians rise, above. Uneasily the soldiers stare up at them.

You – night watch. You, you go with him. You take the East Gate. The rest to quarters. Move!

They disperse. ESTETE *and the priests remain.*

X

DE SOTO (*to* PIZARRO). Mutiny's smoking. Act now or it'll be a blaze you'll not put out.

PIZARRO. What do I do?

DE SOTO. Take our chances, what else can we do? You have to let him go.

PIZARRO. And what happens then? A tiny army is wiped out in five minutes, and the whole story lost for always. Later someone else will conquer Peru and no one will even remember my name.

DE SOTO. What kind of name will they remember if you kill him?

PIZARRO. A conqueror. That at least.

DE SOTO. A man who butchered his prisoner after giving his word. There's a name for your ballads.

PIZARRO. I'll never live to hear them. What do I care? What does it matter? Whatever I do, what does it matter?

DE SOTO. Nothing, if you don't feel it. But I think you do.

PIZARRO. Let me understand you. As Second in Command, you counsel certain death for this army?

DE SOTO. I'll not counsel his.

PIZARRO. Then you counsel the death of Christ in this country, as you told my page boy months ago?

DE SOTO. That's not known.

PIZARRO. As good.

DE SOTO. No. Christ is love. Love is—

PIZARRO. What? *What?*

DE SOTO. Now in him. He trusts you, trust him. It's all you can do.

PIZARRO. Have you gone soft in the head? What's this chorus now? 'Trust! trust!' You know the law out here: kill or get killed. You said it yourself. The mercies come later.

DE SOTO. Not for you. I wish to God you'd never made this bargain. But you did. Now you've no choice left.

PIZARRO. No, this is my kingdom. In Peru I am absolute. I have choice always.

DE SOTO. You had it. But you made it.

PIZARRO. Then I'll take it back.

DE SOTO. Then you never made it. I'm not playing words, General. There's no choice where you don't stick by it.

PIZARRO. I can *choose* to take it back.

DE SOTO. No, sir. That would only be done on orders from your own fear. That's not choosing.

ESTETE. May the Crown be allowed a word?

PIZARRO. I know your word. Death.

ESTETE. What else can it be?

VALVERDE. Your army is in terror. Do you care nothing for them?

PIZARRO. Well, Cavalier. Do you?

DE SOTO. I care for them. But less than I care for you . . . God knows why.

He goes off.

ESTETE. The issue is simple. You are Viceroy here ruling in the name of the King who sent you. You have no right to risk his land for any reason at all.

PIZARRO. And what did this King ever do for me? Granted me salary if I found money to pay it. Allowed me governance if I found land to govern. Magnificent! For years I strove to make this expedition, years of scars and hunger. While I sweated your Holy Roman vulture turned away his beak till I'd shaken out enough gold to tempt his greed. If I'd failed this time he'd have cast me off with one shrug of his royal feathers. Well, now I cast him. Francisco Pizarro casts off Carlos the Fifth. Go and tell him.

ESTETE. This is ridiculous.

PIZARRO. No doubt, but you'll have to give me better argument before I give him up.

ESTETE. Perverse man, what is Atahuallpa to you?

PIZARRO. Someone I promised Life.

ESTETE. Promised life? How quaint. The sort of chivalry idea you pretend to despise. If you want to be an absolute king, my man, you must learn to act out of personal will. Break your word just *because* you gave it. Till then, you're only a pig-man trying to copy his betters.

> PIZARRO *rounds on him angrily.*

VALVERDE. My son, listen to me. No promise to a pagan need bind a Christian. Simply think what's at stake: the lives of a hundred and seventy of the faithful. Are you going to sacrifice them for one savage?

PIZARRO. You know lives have no weight, Father. Ten can't be added up to outbalance one.

VALVERDE. Ten good can against one evil. And this man is evil. His people kiss his hands as the source of life.

PIZARRO. As we do yours. All your days you play at being God. You only hate my Inca because he does it better.

VALVERDE. *What?*

PIZARRO. Dungballs to all churches that are or ever could be! How I hate you. 'Kill who I bid you kill and I will pardon it.' YOU with your milky fingers forcing in the blade. How dare you priests bless any man who goes slicing into battle? But no. You slice with him. 'Rip!' you scream, 'Tear! blind! in the name of Christ!' Tell me soft Father, if Christ was here now, do you think he would kill my Inca? . . . Well, Brother de Nizza, you're the lord of answers: let's hear you. Do I kill him?

DE NIZZA. Don't try and trap me. I know as well as you how terrible it is to kill. But worse is to spare evil. When I came here first I thought I had found Paradise. Now I know it is Hell. A country which castrates its people. What are your Inca's subjects? A population of eunuchs, living entirely without choice.

PIZARRO. And what are your Christians? Unhappy hating men. Look: I'm a peasant, I want value for money. If I go marketing for Gods, who do I buy? The God of Europe with all its death and brooding, or Atahuallpa of Peru?

His spirit keeps an Empire sweet and still as corn in the field.

DENIZZA. And you're content to be a stalk of corn?

PIZARRO. Yes, yes! They're no fools, these sun men. They know what cheats you sell on your barrow. Choice. Hunger. Tomorrow. They've looked at your wares and passed on. They live here as part of nature, no hope and no despair.

DENIZZA. And no life. Why must you be so dishonest? You are not only part of nature, and you know it. There is something in you at war with nature; there is in all of us. Something that does not belong in you the animal. What do you think it is? What is this pain in you that month after month makes you hurl yourself against the cage of time? . . . This is God, driving you to accept divine eternity. Take it, General: not this pathetic copy of eternity the Incas have tried to make on earth. Peru is a sepulchre of the soul. For the sake of the free spirit in each of us it must be destroyed.

PIZARRO. So there is Christian charity. To save my own soul I must kill another man!

DENIZZA. To save love in the world you must kill lovelessness.

PIZARRO. Hail to you, sole judge of love! No salvation outside your church: and no love neither. Oh, your arrogance! . . . (*Simply*) I do not know love, Father, but what can I ever know, if I feel none for him?

DIEGO (*rushing on*). Sir! Sir! Another fight broke out, sir. There's one dead.

PIZARRO. Who?

DIEGO. Blas. He drew a knife. I only meant to spit his leg, but he slipped and got it through the guts.

PIZARRO. You did well to punish fighting.

DIEGO. May I speak free, sir?

PIZARRO. What? I've got to kill him, is that it?

DIEGO. What other way is there? The men are out of their wits. They feel death all round them.

PIZARRO. So it is and let them face it. I promised them gold, not life. Well, they've got gold. The cripples have gold crutches. The coughers spit gold snot. The bargain's over.

DIEGO. No, sir, not with me. To me you're the greatest
General in the world. And we're the greatest company.

PIZARRO. Pizarro's boys, is that it?

DIEGO. Yes, sir. Pizarro's boys.

PIZARRO. Ah, the old band. The dear old regiment. Fool!
Look, you were born a man. Not a Blue man, or a Green
man, but A MAN. You are able to feel a thousand separate
loves unordered by fear or solitude. Are you going to trade
them all in for Gang-love? Flag-love? Carlos-the-Fifth-love?
Jesus-the-Christ-love? All that has been tied on you; it is
only this that makes you bay for death.

VALVERDE. I'll give you death. When I get back to Spain,
a commission will hale you to the stake for what you have
said today.

PIZARRO. If I let the Inca go, Father, you'll never get back
to Spain.

ESTETE. You madman: see here, you put him underground
by sunset or I'll take the knife to him myself.

PIZARRO. ATAHUALLPA!

ATAHUALLPA *enters with* YOUNG MARTIN.

They ache for your death. They want to write psalms to
their God in your blood. But they'll all die before you –
that I promise. (*He binds* ATAHUALLPA'S *arm to his
own with a long cord of rope last used to tie some gold.*)
There. No, no, come here. Now no one will kill you unless
they kill me first.

ESTETE. De Candia!

Enter DE CANDIA, *with a drawn sword.*

DE CANDIA. A touching game – gaolers and prisoners. But
it's over now. General, do you think I'm going to die so
that you can dance with a darkie?

PIZARRO *pulls the sword from* YOUNG MARTIN'S
scabbard.

DIEGO (*drawing*). Sorry sir, but it's got to be done.

ESTETE (*drawing*). There's nothing you can do, Pizarro. The
whole camp's against you.

PIZARRO. De Soto!

DE CANDIA. If de Soto raises his sword, he'll lose the arm that swings it.

PIZARRO. You'll lose yours first. Come on!

He rushes at DE CANDIA *but* ATAHUALLPA *gives a growl and pulls him back by the rope. A pause.*

ATAHUALLPA. I have no eyes for you. You are nothing.

PIZARRO. I command here still. They will obey me.

ATAHUALLPA. They will kill me though you cry curses of earth and sky. (*To them all*) Leave us. I will speak with him.

Impressed by the command in his voice, all leave, save the General – now roped to his prisoner – and YOUNG MARTIN.

XI

ATAHUALLPA. It is no matter. They cannot kill me.

PIZARRO. Cannot?

ATAHUALLPA. Man who dies cannot kill a God who lives forever.

PIZARRO. I wouldn't bet on it, my lord.

ATAHUALLPA. Only my father can take me from here. And he would not accept me killed by men like you. Men with no word. You may be King in this land, but never God. I am God of the Four Quarters and if you kill me tonight I will rise at dawn when my Father first touches my body with light.

PIZARRO. You believe this?

ATAHUALLPA. All my people know it – it is why they have let me stay with you.

PIZARRO. They knew you could not be harmed . . .

ATAHUALLPA. So.

PIZARRO. Was this the meaning? The meaning of my dream? You were choosing me?

YOUNG MARTIN. My lord, it's just a boast. Beyond any kind of reason.

PIZARRO. Is it?

YOUNG MARTIN. How can a man die, then get up and walk away?

PIZARRO. Let's hear your creed, boy. 'I believe in Jesus Christ, the Son of God, that He suffered under Pontius Pilate, was crucified, dead and buried' . . . and what?

YOUNG MARTIN. Sir?

PIZARRO. What?

YOUNG MARTIN. 'He descended into Hell, and on the third day He rose again from the dead . . .'

PIZARRO. You don't believe it!

YOUNG MARTIN. I do! On my soul! I believe with perfect faith!

PIZARRO. But Christ's to be the only one, is that it? What if it's possible, here in a land beyond all maps and scholars, guarded by mountains up to the sky, that there were true Gods on earth, creators of true peace? Think of it! Gods, free of time.

YOUNG MARTIN. It's impossible, my lord.

PIZARRO. It's the only way to give life meaning! To blast out of time and live forever, *us*, in our own persons. This is the law: die in despair or be a God yourself! . . . Look at him: always so calm as if the teeth of life never bit him . . . or the teeth of death. What if it was really true, Martin? That I've gone God-hunting and caught one. A being who can renew his life over and over?

YOUNG MARTIN. But how can he do that, sir? How could any man?

PIZARRO. By returning over and over again to the source of life – *to the Sun*!

YOUNG MARTIN. No, sir . . .

PIZARRO. Why not? What else is a God but what we know we can't do without? The flowers that worship it, the sun-flowers in their soil, are us after night, after cold and light-less days, turning our faces to it, adoring. The sun is the only God I know! We eat you to walk. We drink you to sing. Our reins loosen under you and we laugh. Even I laugh, here!

YOUNG MARTIN. General, you need rest, sir.

Pause.

PIZARRO. Yes. Yes . . . yes. (*Bitterly*) How clever. He's understood everything I've said to him these awful months – all my secret pain he's heard – and this is his revenge. This futile joke. How he must hate me. (*Tightening the rope*) Oh, yes, you cunning bastard! Look, Martin – behold, my God. I've got the Sun on a string! I can make it rise: (*He pulls the Inca's arm up*) – or set! *He throws the Inca to his knees.*

YOUNG MARTIN. General . . . !

PIZARRO. I'll make you set forever! Two can joke as well as one. You want your freedom? All right, you're free! (*He starts circling round* ATAHUALLPA) Walk out of the camp! They may stop you, but what's that to you? You're invulnerable. They'll knock you down but your father the Sun will pick you up again. Go on! Get up! . . . Go on! . . . Get up! . . . Go on! . . . Go on! . . . Go on! . . . Go on! . . . Go on! . . . Go on!

> *He breaks into a frantic gallop round and round the Inca, the rope at full stretch,* ATAHUALLPA *turning with him, somersaulting, then holding him, his teeth bared with the strain, as if breaking a wild horse, until the old man tumbles exhausted to the ground. Silence follows, broken only by deep moaning from the stricken man. Quietly the Inca pulls in the rope. Then at last he speaks.*

ATAHUALLPA. Pizarro. You will die soon and you do not believe in your God. That is why you tremble and keep no word. Believe in me. I will give you a word and fill you with joy. For you I will do a great thing. I will swallow death and spit it out of me.   *poetic metaphor*

Pause. This whole scene stays very still.

PIZARRO (*whispering*). You cannot.

ATAHUALLPA. Yes, if my father wills it.

PIZARRO. How if he does not?

ATAHUALLPA. He will. His people still need me. Believe.

PIZARRO. Impossible.

ATAHUALLPA. Believe.

PIZARRO. How? . . . How? . . .

ATAHUALLPA. First you must take my priest power.

PIZARRO (*quietly*). Oh, no! you go or not as you choose,
but I take nothing more in this world.

ATAHUALLPA. Take my word. Take my peace. I will put
water to your wound, old man. Believe.

> *A long silence. The lights are now fading round
> them.*

PIZARRO. What must I do?

> *Enter* OLD MARTIN.

OLD MARTIN. How can I speak now and hope to be believed? As night fell like a hand over the eye, and great
white stars sprang out over the snow-rim of our world, Atahuallpa confessed Pizarro. He did it in the Inca manner.
He took Ichu grass and a stone. Into the Ichu grass the
General spoke for an hour or more. None heard what he
said save the King, who could not understand it. Then the
King struck him on the back with the stone, cast away
the grass, and made the signs for purification.

PIZARRO. If any blessing is in me, take it and go. Fly up,
my bird, and come to me again.

> *The* INCA *takes a knife from* YOUNG MARTIN *and
> cuts the rope. Then he walks upstage. All the*
> OFFICERS *and* MEN *enter. During the following
> a pole is set up above, in the sun, and* ATAHUALLPA
> *is hauled up into it.*

XII

OLD MARTIN. The Inca was tried by a court quickly mustered. He was accused of usurping the throne and killing
his brother; of idolatry and of having more than one wife.
On all these charges he was found—

ESTETE. Guilty.

VALVERDE. Guilty.

DE CANDIA. Guilty.

DIEGO. Guilty.

OLD MARTIN. Sentence to be carried out the same night.

ESTETE. Death by burning.

Lights up above the sun.

ATAHUALLPA *gives a great cry.*

PIZARRO. No! He must not burn! His body must stay in one piece.

VALVERDE. Let him repent his idolatry and be baptized a Christian. He will receive the customary mercy.

OLD MARTIN. Strangling instead.

PIZARRO. You must do it! Deny your Father! If you don't, you will be burnt to ashes. There will be no flesh left for him to warm alive at dawn.

YOUNG MARTIN *screams and runs from the stage in horror.*

You must do it.

In a gesture of surrender the Inca king kneels.

OLD MARTIN. So it was that Atahuallpa came to Christ.

Enter DE NIZZA, *above, with a bowl of water.*

DE NIZZA. I baptise you Juan de Atahuallpa, in honour of Juan the Baptist, whose sacred day this is. –1 impossible

ESTETE. The twenty-ninth of August 1533.

VALVERDE. And may Our Lord and His angels receive your soul with joy!

SOLDIERS. Amen!

The Inca suddenly raises his head, tears off his clothes and intones in a great voice:

ATAHUALLPA. INTI! INTI! INTI!

VALVERDE. What does he say?

PIZARRO (*intoning also*). The Sun. The Sun. The Sun.

VALVERDE. *Kill him!*

Soldiers haul ATAHUALLPA *to his feet and hold him to the stake.* RODAS *slips a string over his head and while all the Spaniards recite the Latin Creed below, and great howls of 'Inca!' come from the darkness, the Sovereign King of Peru is garrotted. His screams and struggles subside; his body falls slack. His executioners hand the corpse down to the soldiers below, who carry it to the centre of the stage and drop*

cruel

77

it at PIZARRO'S *feet. Then all leave save the old man, who stands as if turned to stone. A drum beats. Slowly, in semi-darkness, the stage fills with all the Indians, robed in black and terracotta, wearing the great golden funeral masks of ancient Peru. Grouped round the prone body, they intone a strange Chant of Resurrection, punctuated by hollow beats on the drums and by long, long silences in which they turn their immense triangular eyes enquiringly up to the sky. Finally, after three great cries appear to summon it, the sun rises. Its rays fall on the body.* ATA-HUALLPA *does not move. The masked men watch in amazement – disbelief – finally, despair. Slowly, with hanging, dejected heads, they shuffle away.* PIZARRO *is left alone with the dead King. He contemplates him. A silence. Then suddenly he slaps it viciously, and the body rolls over on its back.*

PIZARRO. Cheat! You've cheated me! Cheat . . .

For a moment his old body is racked with sobs; then, surprised, he feels tears on his cheek. He examines them. The sunlight brightens on his head.

What's this? What is it? In all your life you never made one of these, I know, and I not till this minute. Look. (*He kneels to show the dead Inca*) Ah, no. You have no eyes for me now, Atahuallpa: they are dusty balls of amber I can tap on. You have no peace for me, Atahuallpa: the birds still scream in your forest. You have no joy for me, Atahuallpa, my boy: the only joy is in death. I lived between two hates: I die between two darks: blind eyes and a blind sky. And yet you saw once. The sky sees nothing, but you saw. Is their comfort there? The sky knows no feeling, but we know them, that's sure. Martin's hope, and de Soto's honour, and your trust – your trust which hunted me: we alone make these. That's some marvel, yes, some marvel. To sit in a great cold silence, and sing out sweet with just our own warm breath: that's some marvel, surely. To make water in a sand world: surely, surely . . . God's just a name on your nail; and

78

naming begins cries and cruelties. But to live without hope of after, and make whatever God there is, oh, that's some immortal business surely . . . I'm tired. Where are you? You're so cold. I'd warm you if I could. But there's no warming now, not ever now. I'm colding too. There's a snow of death falling all round us. You can almost see it. It's over, lad, I'm coming after you. There's nothing but peace to come. We'll be put into the same earth, father and son in our own land. And that sun will roam uncaught over his empty pasture.

OLD MARTIN. So fell Peru. We gave her greed, hunger and the Cross: three gifts for the civilized life. The family groups that sang on the terraces are gone. In their place slaves shuffle underground and they don't sing there. Peru is a silent country, frozen in avarice. So fell Spain, gorged with gold; distended; now dying.

remonument

PIZARRO (*singing*). 'Where is her heart, O little finch' . . .

OLD MARTIN. And so fell you, General, my master, whom men called the Son of His Own Deeds. He was killed later in a quarrel with his partner who brought up the reinforcements. But to speak truth, he sat down that morning and never really got up again.

PIZARRO (*singing*). 'Where are her plumes, O little finch' . . .

OLD MARTIN. I'm the only one left now of that company: landowner – slaveowner – and forty years from any time of hope. It put out a good blossom, but it was shaken off rough. After that I reckon the fruit always comes sour, and doesn't sweeten up much with age.

PIZARRO (*singing*). 'She is cut up, O little finch. For stealing grain, O little finch' . . .

OLD MARTIN. General, you did for me, and now I've done for you. And there's no joy in that. Or in anything now. But then there's no joy in the world could match for me what I had when I first went with you across the water to find the gold country. And no pain like losing it. Save you all.

He goes out. PIZARRO *lies beside the body of*

ATAHUALLPA *and quietly sings to it.*
PIZARRO (*singing*).
> See, see the fate, O little finch,
> Of robber birds, O little finch.

The sun glares at the audience.

heroics

(excellente)

SCHEDULE OF MUSIC

LIST OF MUSIC IN SCORE

1. Recorded Organ Music (4 min. 45 sec.)
2. Opening of the Sun (35-40 sec.) – orchestra and chants
3. End of the Court scene (15-45 sec.) – orchestral
4. Atahuallpa's invitation to Pizarro – orchestral
5. The bird cries in the forest (up to 6 min.) – 4 tracks of recorded bird cries plus Indians on 'bird flutes' and guerros
6. Introduction to 'Toil Song' – orchestral
7. 'Toil Song' – Indian singing with small marracas and small drum
8. Villac Umu's Embassy: arrival (5 sec.)
   exit (5 sec.) } orchestral
9. Indian Chants of Praise – orchestra and chants
10. Offstage Spanish Te Deum – recorded Spanish chanting
11. Climbing of the Andes (up to 6 min.) – orchestral (2 flexatons)
12. Procession into Cajamarca (1 min.-1 min. 20 sec.) – orchestra, plus Indians playing bells, cymbals, 'thumb pianos', marracas (large)
13. The Massacre (1 min.-1 min. 30 sec.) – orchestra plus bells on Indians
14. 1st Indian Lament – chant
15. Atahuallpa's Command for Gold (35 sec.) – orchestral
16. Clothing of Atahuallpa and his meal – Indians hum and play crotales, 'musical plates' and 'thumb pianos'
17. 1st Gold Procession – orchestra plus Indian humming
18. 'Little Finch' song – Atahuallpa sings
19. 2nd Gold Procession – orchestra plus Indian humming
20. The Dice Scene – orchestra plus Indian menaces; Indians play bird flutes and guerros
21. The Garotting of Atahuallpa – orchestra
22. Indian Chants of Resurrection – orchestra and chants

INSTRUMENTATION OF SCORE
(Orchestra: four percussionists)

Indians play the following on stage
   2 drums (Indian 'tablas' or 2 pairs of bongos)
   2 suspended cymbals on 'Indian handles'
   2 pairs very large marracas
   1 pair very small marracas on long handles
   4 guerros

81

2 dozen bamboo 'bird flutes' (slide recorders) (these can be obtained from any shop specializing in folk craft from India)

2 'thumb pianos' (cigar box type sounding board with spring steel tongues which should be hit with light, hard sticks)

Orchestral instruments, divided between four percussion players

6 suspended cymbals
4 pairs of bongos
1 big drum
1 xylophone
1 glockenspiel
2 lion roar drums (string drums)
2 guerros
5 triangles
3 pairs crotales (small cymbals)
2 sets of sleigh bells
1 woodblock
4 slapsticks
1 large flexaton (musical saw; blade approximately 5 ft. 6 in. long)
1 small flexaton

THE MASSACRE

All Indians have small bells sewn along their sleeves in the Massacre (and the Procession into Cajamarca). Insofar as their movements are rhythmed, and in time with the orchestral music, this helps to keep the centre of musical (as well as dramatic) attention on stage. There is a section in the orchestral score of the Massacre which is almost completely silent, to enhance this effect.

THE BIRD CRIES IN THE FOREST (1st Act)

THE DICE SCENE (*Ruminagui*) (2nd Act)

In both these scenes the Indians play loud interjections to word cues on both 'bird flutes' and guerros, as a counterpart either to the recording of bird cries, or the orchestral music, to bring closer the sense of threat and danger to the centre of dramatic attention.

TOIL SONG

Schedule of Music

As the Indians come on the stage they all hum this tune, accompanied by the two women, one woman playing small marracas (one marraca to each beat), the other beating the exact rhythm on a small drum (perhaps a 'tabla' wood drum). When work commences the two women sing the song twice, then all resume humming as the Spaniards speak until all workers are off stage.

LITTLE FINCH

This should be sung very simply with no 'rubato'. Accentuation and dynamics must depend on the meaning of the words. The glissandi should be as the swooping of a bird of prey.

THE HUMMINGS

Atahuallpa's Dressing Scene and meal:

All Indians should hum this tune throughout the scene.

The Indians who help to dress Atahuallpa all have one pair of suspended crotales (ancient Chinese cymbals) hanging from each wrist (about 15 inches of string to each crotale). The Indians who bring on food and feed Atahuallpa have no crotales, but the gold plates should have many small bells hanging below the rims. The plates should also have double bottoms (the lower ones are drum skins). Dried peas or gravel should be inserted between the two bottoms, thus turning the plates into rattles. These plates should be 'played' as they are carried onstage and until Atahuallpa receives his first morsel of food. During Atahuallpa's meal, plates and crotales are silent, the humming continues accompanied by two 'thumb pianos' (pitch ad libitum, to the rhythm of the 'Toil song')

THE GOLD PROCESSIONS

Hum the TOIL SONG at a lower pitch, *slow*.

Glossary: reading the text

Characters in the play

Royal Veedor, Or Overseer   The King's representative, supervising events on his behalf.

Dominican   preaching friar of the order of St Dominic.

Franciscan Friar   preaching friar of the order of St Francis of Assisi.

Act 1, scene 1

1 *four black crucifixes, sharpened to resemble swords*   Shaffer's setting hints, from the outset, at the link between religion and force. The crucifixes here obviously symbolise the Christian religion, but their colour and position also create a strong sense of menace.

grizzled   having grey hair.

hidalgo   nobleman.

Save you all   God save you all.

counting house   bank.

impetuous   acting hastily, without thought.

2 *Don Chistobal on the rules of Chivalry*   this mediaeval book taught knights the correct code of conduct: this included courage, honour, a sense of justice and a readiness to help the weak.

Viceroy   ruler on behalf of the King.

3 *page*   boy in training to be a knight.

slogger   hard worker.

mercenary   soldier fighting abroad in pursuit of money rather than belief in a cause.

4 *Chaplain*   clergyman attached to the army.

Cavalier knight.

Cordoba (died 1518) Spanish soldier and explorer.

llama beast of the camel family, hairy and without a hump. The Incas considered it sacred.

Balboa leader of an expedition which discovered the Pacific Ocean in 1513.

aloe plant with toothed leaves and red or yellow flowers.

farrier someone who looks after horses.

treacherous and hysterical dangerously unreliable and prone to emotional outbursts.

stupefied astonished.

demure reserved, serious.

5 *absolve* pardon.

pissing mildly obscene word used throughout the play to indicate even stronger language.

cooper barrel-maker.

6 *muster* recruiting ceremony.

lodestone attraction (something that is magnetic).

7 *my father couldn't own to my mother* Pizarro was born illegitimate.

arquebus portable long-barrelled gun.

---

1 What are your first impressions of Pizarro? How do the other characters behave towards him?

2 Apart from a search for gold, what other reasons can you see for the mission?

3 What is the importance of the narrator in this first scene?

Act 1, scene 2

8 *austere polyphony* simple music made up of several melodies played at the same time.

Franciscan see note to 'Characters in the play' (page 84).

serene peaceful.

Venetian belonging to the republic of Venice.

stealth extreme care.

consecrated blessed.

muster strength.

affliction suffering.

9 *tumbled* disorganised.

ginger eager.

haughty arrogant.

Veedor see note to 'Characters in the play' (page 84).

10 *Dungballs* another word used throughout the play in place of other obscenities, meaning nonsense.

A colt...sightless track a young horse trained to run wearing blinkers along its course.

---

1 Why is there tension between Pizarro and Estete?

2 What does Young Martin learn about soldiering from Pizarro?

3 Does Pizarro aim to encourage or dissuade Young Martin from accompanying him?

Act 1, scene 3

11 *'Inca!'* as well as the name for the people, the word also means the ruler or king of the empire.

formalized artificial.

terracotta   brownish-orange colour.

prostrate   flatten themselves to the ground in worship.

12 *Chasqui*   messenger.

The White God returns!   the Inca people believed that their great god of creation, Viracocha, would return one day in white.

Ware You!   beware.

Cuzco   capital city of the Inca's empire in central Peru.

Capac   chief.

---

1   The mood of this scene changes abruptly. How is this achieved?

2   What effects enable Atahuallpa to appear *Godlike* in this scene?

3   Why does Atahuallpa command his court to cover their mouths?

Act 1, scene 4

mottled   blotches of various colours.

12 *horde*   vast crowd.

God's wounds   oath referring to the wounds Christ suffered at crucifixion.

13 *stylized*   unnatural.

not-wife   mistress (the language of the Incas contains no single word to express this).

Sapa Inca! Inca Capac!   the only god! Sovereign god!

14 *Anti-Christ*   the enemy of Christ, expected by early Christians to reign over the world until Christ's second coming.

shift his soul   convert him.

rigour   strictness.

idolatry   worshipping of images.

pagan   heathen, irreligious.

15 *prophesy* prediction .

The twelfth Lord...Four Quarters the present Inca emperor, Atahuallpa, is the twelfth ruler of the entire world (which is divided into four quarters).

> 1 What is Atahuallpa's attitude towards the advancing Spanish and their God?
>
> 2 What impression do you imagine the soldiers have made on the Indians?

Act 1, scene 5

15 *been had* deceived.

16 *cut us out* i.e. out of our armour.

arquebus see note to page 7.

Strozzi famous gun-maker of Florence.

brownies racist term used by the Spanish throughout the play to describe the Inca people.

Venetian the people of Venice were considered to be concerned chiefly with making money.

collective common, shared.

Byzantium city in Ancient Greece.

castrated made sexless, like angels.

immortal everlasting.

17 *condor* a large vulture.

legitimates people with two married parents.

gobbets scraps of raw flesh.

harry annoy.

---

1 Why does Pizzaro provoke fear in De Candia?

2 What does Pizarro mean when he says to Young Martin: *you own everything I lost?*

3 What does Pizarro mean by the analogy *The eagle rips the condor; the condor rips the crow. And the crow would blind all the eagles in the sky if once it had the beak to do it?*

Act 1, scene 6

18 *mimosa*   tropical shrub with yellow flowers.

20 *tupu*   approximately an acre.

we are born greedy   since Adam's sin, according to the Catholic faith, humans have been afflicted with greed.

covetousness   desire to own another person's possessions or property.

four great roads   all leading in from the corners of the empire to the capital.

22 *garrison*   base for troops.

---

1 How is the Indians' way of life structured differently from that of the Spaniards?

2 Technically, how has the audience been able to receive Atahuallpa's response to the action at the same time as Pizarro's when – within the same context of the play – they are physically separate?

Act 1, scene 7

22 *pelts*   rushes.

We're the eggs and...stew   we're the first course and you're the main course.

23 *Lent Procession* parade of images to commemorate Christ's death; the carved faces of the figures appear calm and indifferent to suffering.

cheeseworms maggots in the soldiers' food.

pig-boy see page 7: Pizarro talks of his childhood among pigs. His first words in the play introduce his shame at being 'suckled by a sow' and raised in a pig-sty (page 2).

24 *Zaran...Motupe* two villages.

Viracochian Aticsi Praise Viracocha (the father of the Sun).

Caylla int'i cori praise the son of the sun.

Huachha Cuyak! friend of the powerless.

---

1 How does Pizarro boost the confidence of his soldiers?

2 Why won't Atahuallpa take Villac Umu's advice?

Act 1, scene 8

25 *lugging* pulling.

skittery unsteady and nervous.

26 *pricked* sensitive.

27 *blasphemy* irreligious comments.

usurp take over.

---

1 Why does Pizarro send the message that he too is a God?

2 How do you imagine Valverde receives the comment that it is all right to usurp Christ's name for a night in order to conquer in His name?

Act 1, scene 9

27 *eucalyptus*   large evergreen trees.

Brace up   prepare yourself.

28 *Lowers the odds*   increases our chances.

29 *San Jago*   Spanish name for St James.

Holy Virgin...Conception   Roman Catholics pray to the Virgin Mary, in different images, to mediate with Christ for them. Diego suggests that he might switch his prayers to a different image of her (i.e to the Virgin of the Conception) if she does not help them.

---

1   Why does Pizarro's attitude to Young Martin soften at this point?

2   Why is a sword important to Martin? What does it stand for?

Act 1, scene 10

31 *maggoty*   full of maggots (the larva of insects).

go with Time   accept time's power to change.

dandled   bounced.

32 *soothsayer*   prophet.

emblem   symbol.

---

1   What is the significance of the pause at the top of page 32 after De Soto replies to Pizarro that there is death in everything except God?

2   Why is this particular morning significant to Pizarro?

Act 1, scene 11

33 *Exsurge Domine* (Latin) Rise up, O Lord (from the Psalms).

Deus meus…peccatoris deliver me, my God, from the hands of the sinner.

Many strong bulls…dust of death images from Psalm 22.

cleaves sticks.

34 *an omen* sign of a future happening.

35 *the Apocalypse* the last book of the Bible gives a vivid, terrifying account of the end of the world. It includes the prophesy that prior to the Second Coming of Christ the earth will be ruled by the wicked.

teems is crowded with.

36 *Save you* God save you.

---

1 Dramatically, how has the tension of waiting been achieved?
2 Is Pizarro right to betray Atahuallpa?

Act 1, scene 12

36 *marraccas* percussion instruments: shells containing seeds which can create a rhythm when shaken.

embossed fixed upon.

37 *pagan* see note to page 14.

expound explain.

Regent ruler serving on behalf of the king or (as here) God.

vassal servant who is entirely dependent on his master.

38 *SAN JAGO Y CIERRA ESPAÑA* Spanish war cry meaning 'St James and close Spain' (close Spain to the invaders).

hew cut.

quarry   victims.

bellies   swells.

---

1   Why do you think Peter Shaffer uses the device of Old and Young
    Martin on stage? What are the advantages and disadvantages of the
    technique?

2   How is the personality of Young Martin quite different from that of Old
    Martin?

3   Why has Shaffer chosen to depict the greater massacre in mime?

4   What does the blood-stained cloth symbolise?

Act 2, scene 1

39   *lament is intoned*   song of sorrow is sung.

new spurs   presented as a sign of having achieved the status of knight.

40   *butlers*   head servants.

defiled   raped.

---

1   How does De Soto justify the killings?

2   Young Martin doesn't understand what De Soto means by the phrase
    I must be Winter for our Lord to be Spring. What do you imagine it
    implies?

Act 2, scene 2

40   *serene arrogance*   peaceful sense of superiority.

41   *rue*   regret.

42   *thirty and three*   Jesus Christ was around this age when he was killed.

1 In what ways does Felipillo demonstrate his untrustworthiness in this scene?

2 How does Young Martin's attitude towards Atahuallpa contrast with those around him?

Act 2, scene 3

43 *pyxes* sacred boxes in which the wafers for communion are kept.

What are the poor? Inca civilisation included a welfare system to care for the needy.

Two showings of my Mother Moon two months.

44 *niceties* tiny details.

Alexander, Tamberlaine previous conquerors.

lodestone see note to page 6.

45 *ceilings of death* ceilings of tombs.

Quito northern town.

Pachamacac shrine of the god Pachamacac.

Cuzco capital city of the empire.

Coricancha part of the Temple at Cuzco. It has walls of gold.

Vilcanota…Colae…Aymaraes and Arequipa various temples.

Chimu a nothern Inca tribe.

1 Does evidence from this scene indicate that Atahuallpa is a good leader?

2 Why does Atahuallpa decide to make a deal with the Spaniards?

Act 2, scene 4

46 *to audience*   to talk with.

reverence   respect.

turquoises   greenish-blue gemstones.

garnished with   decorated with.

48 *he becomes a biscuit*   for Roman Catholics the wafer used in Mass, once
blessed, is transformed into the body of Christ.

50 *fretted*   decorated with angular designs.

pesos   Spanish coins.

rising   uprising, rebellion.

51 *slack*   freedom.

---

1   Why is it appropriate for the cloth of blood to be removed at this point?
2   Compare and contrast the Inca philosophy with the Spanish
philosophy.

Act 2, scene 5

52 *smoking wood*   unclear and difficult to interpret.

53 *My Sky Father*   the Sun, Inti.

suckled by a sow   see note to page 23.

54 *aylu*   translated in the next line by Young Martin.

litheness   suppleness.

---

1   Why do you think Pizarro is developing so much respect for
Atahuallpa?
2   What does Atahuallpa possess or represent that Pizarro lacks in his
life?

Act 2, scene 6

55 *halberd*   spear fitted with an axe head.

56 *limepit*   grave.

easy   relaxed.

57 *Arabs*   Arabian horses, bred to race.

58 *breach*   disobeying the commands.

---

1   What does the assault on the sun symbolise?

2   Why does Diego feel that it will be necessary for Atahuallpa to be killed?

3   In what respects has the sense of danger heightened?

Act 2, scene 7

58 *hidalgo*   see note to page 1.

on the turn   becoming rebellious.

60 *avenge them*   get revenge on behalf of them.

61 *gloat*   to feel smug, or highly satisfied with oneself.

62 *disdain*   dislike.

63 *curdle*   dry up.

vicuna   animal similar to the llama yielding fine wool.

dote on   love to an extreme degree.

stalking   hunting.

anguish   suffering.

---

1   How does Atahuallpa's attitude towards Pizarro change in this scene?

2   Is Atahuallpa making the right decision in not accepting Pizarro's conditions?

Act 2, scene 8

64 *booty*   treasure.

Genoa…Milan…Rome   Italian cities.

fops   men who are obsessed with fashion.

65 *tunnel*   backside.

So the Palace…after all   the Court, having tried to seem uninvolved in events, now owns up to its dark motives.

What effect does De Candia have on the already tense situation?

Act 2, scene 9

66 *morale*   good spirits (of the army).

the frozen boy   Atahuallpa.

67 *Ruminagui*   one of Atahuallpa's generals.

---

1   What is the significance of the bird references in this and the previous scenes?

2   Why do you imagine Atahuallpa continues not to resist the Spaniards' oppression?

Act 2, scene 10

68 *Mutiny's smoking*   rebellion is brewing.

ballads   songs.

counsel   advise.

69 *absolute*   completely in charge.

Perverse   unnatural.

70 *castrates its subjects*   removes the power of its people.

   eunuchs   castrated men.

71 *cheats*   frauds, lies.

   sepulchre   tomb.

72 *hale*   drag.

   stake   form of torture where the person is tied to a post, often for expressing irreligious views.

---

1   What has contributed to De Soto's change in attitude towards Atahuallpa?

2   What do you think is Pizarro's responsibility as the King's Viceroy at this point in the action?

Act 2, scene 11

74 *Christ's*   resurrection from the dead.

   our reins loosen   under the sun the restrictions on our lives seem fewer.

75 *futile*   pointless.

   somersaulting   turning head over heels.

   stricken   injured.

76 *Ichu grass*   coarse grass.

To what extent does Young Martin act as Pizarro's conscience in this scene?

Act 2, scene 12

mustered   gathered together.

idolatry   see note to page 14.

77 *garrotted*   killed by strangling and breaking of the neck.

    amber   orange resin used in ornaments.

79 *avarice*   extreme greed.

---

1 Why is Valverde determined to baptise Atahuallpa?

2 How would you describe Old Martin's feelings at the end of the play?

3 What has his relationship with Atahuallpa taught Pizarro?

4 In what ways does the death of Atahuallpa remind you of the death of Christ?

5 What does the play suggest about religious belief?

■ Study programme

Characters

1. • In groups of three or four, gather information about Pizarro's past from the text. You will find that much of it is provided by Pizarro himself, in Act 1, scene 10, for example.

   • 'Freeze-frame' any significant moments from Pizarro's past that have been described in the text. Do they help to explain why he has become the character he projects?

   • Share your freeze-frame with the rest of the class and discuss what you discovered about Pizarro.

2. Working in groups of four or more, read the chief's account of Atahuallpa's origins on page 13 and piece together his life before the action of the play. Relate the story using appropriate language and movement. Try and capture the style the chief has adopted.

3. Working in pairs:
   • write a list of words that describe Atahuallpa;
   • write a list of words that describe Pizarro.

   Share your findings.

4. Working in pairs, select an extract from the play that illustrates a growing warmth and understanding between Pizarro and Atahuallpa. Contrast it with earlier encounters where tension was evident.

   Discuss the progression of their relationship and identify why the changes occur.

5. Reviewing the 1964 Chichester Festival Theatre production of *The Royal Hunt of the Sun*, B A Young wrote:

Although Francisco Pizarro has no belief in the code of chivalry he would not break his promise to the Inca Atahuallpa of Peru, whose land he had conquered and robbed, because he found that they were fundamentally two of a kind.

What do you think is meant by this statement? Find evidence in the text to support your views.

Discuss your findings.

6 As a group, discuss the following questions:
- What does the role of Old Martin contribute, apart from narration?
- What factors would need to be taken into consideration when casting the roles of Old and Young Martin?

Style and themes in the play

1 Peter Shaffer has agreed to answer questions about his play. What three key questions would you like to ask him? Examples of things you could ask him about are:
- the reasons for choosing the subject of the play;
- use of a narrator;
- type of language in the play;
- use of many short scenes.

Write down your three questions and pass them to a partner. Try to construct answers to your partner's questions and then discuss them together.

2 As a whole group, discuss how the priests and the Roman Catholic Church in general are presented in the play. What judgement does the play invite us to make on the Church?

3 In groups of four, read Act 1, scene 3. Study the language, how the

language is used with movement, and the style of delivery. Act out the scene with all the characters wearing masks.

- Do masks affect the way the actors play their parts?
- Why do you think Peter Shaffer introduced them?

Performance projects

1. Old Martin suggests that even the youngest soldier saw *himself with a following of Indians and a province for an orchard* (Act 1, scene 2). Create a scene that demonstrates how Pizarro might hope to see himself established in Peru. Your scene should illustrate what you imagine Pizarro hopes to gain from the mission, both for his country and for himself.

2. Working in pairs, with one person playing Old Martin and the other playing a friend, prepare a scene where the friend asks Old Martin how he thinks the massacre of the Incas and Atahuallpa's death could have been prevented.

   Share these scenes with the rest of the class.

3. Working in groups of four, create an alternative ending for the play. Include in your presentation as many theatrical conventions found in *The Royal Hunt of the Sun* as possible – for example, the use of Old Martin as narrator.

4. Choose a scene where the role of the narrator Old Martin is important. Replace Old Martin with an alternative narrator. Choose someone who is likely to have a very different perspective of events. Rewrite the scene with the new narrator and then act it out with a partner, or in a small group.

5. Make a list of the essential qualities which an actor playing the part of Atahuallpa would need to demonstrate.

Role play

1.   *What a fantastic wonder that anyone on earth should dare to say: 'That's my father. My father: the sun!' It's silly – but tremendous… You know – strange nonsense: since first I heard of him I've dreamed of him every night.*

Act 1, scene 10

In groups of four, improvise what you imagine Pizarro sees in his dreams.

2. Read Act 1, scene 12, up until Pizarro's entrance. Each take the character of one of the Spaniards and write an account of this scene and your first impressions of Atahuallpa.

3. • As a whole group, form a circle. Imagine that you are Atahuallpa's court. In role, out of hearing of your Sun King, discuss how you feel about Atahuallpa's response to the advancing Spaniards.

   • In groups of three, discuss what advice you would like to have offered Atahuallpa in Act 1 if the situation had presented itself.

4. • As a whole group, in role as the Inca Indians, imagine that you have been instructed to rehearse the resurrection ceremony. It is some time since it was devised and there is the possibility that you might be called on to perform it. Discuss what experience you have had of it in the past.

   • In groups of five, look at the directions outlined in Act 2, scene 12 (page 76) and improvise the ceremony. Incorporate the various elements that build atmosphere, such as drumbeats and silence. Have someone volunteer to play Atahuallpa so that the scene described can be recreated up to the point where the masked figures shuffle away.

   • Working in pairs, one person take the role of an Inca who was part of the ceremony and the other an Inca who was not a witness to it. The witness should relate the events to the person who was not there.

- Still in roles, discuss what you imagine the future will be following the death of Atahuallpa.

5 Imagine a court of enquiry has been set up in Spain. Its brief is to consider whether Pizarro is guilty of mishandling the mission. Witnesses who accompanied him on the mission are to be called to give evidence.

Approximately five volunteers should take on the roles of the appropriate witnesses. While they discuss the sort of questions they might be called on to answer, the remainder of the group take on the roles of court members and plan questions for the witnesses. Each court member should ask at least one question.

6 The Inca way of life is described in Act 1, scene 6. Taking this as a starting point, imagine you are part of the Indian community before the arrival of the Spaniards.

- Describe what relationship you have to one another and what activity you might be involved in. Take about five minutes to make these decisions through improvisation.

- Develop your improvisation by having one member of your group arrive with the news that strangers have arrived in your land. Improvise how the news affects the group.

- Imagine that – as Incas – you have been told to collect together all your gold and that it must be handed over to the Spaniards without resistance. How do you receive this announcement? What do you decide to do?

Extension assignments

1 What questions would Pizarro have asked his superior before his mission? Working in pairs, improvise an imaginary exchange of views that shows what would have been expected of Pizarro and the army he is to command.

2. Pizarro is about to involve himself in a mission that is not without danger. What sort of preparations do you imagine he would have made?

Perhaps this preparation might include letters to certain associates giving them instructions of what to do should he not return. Or perhaps his letters might have been of a more personal nature. Write one such letter in the style in which Pizarro might have dictated it (he was not literate).

3. Working in pairs, imagine that there is an additional scene between Act 2, scene 2 and scene 3. In it Atahuallpa seeks advice on how to compose himself before his next meeting with Pizarro after an unfortunate first encounter. What sort of dialogue might occur between Atahuallpa and his conscience / his father, the Sun?

4. • Working in pairs, one person take the part of Manco and the other person the part of a runner from the farthest province. What news do you think the runner has to report concerning the Spanish advance through Peruvian territory? Decide how the news should be delivered and received.

• 'Freeze-frame' what you imagine the runner has seen. Share your work with the rest of the class and either discuss what sort of impressions the Incas might have of the advancing Spaniards or 'hotseat' volunteers prepared to give the Incas' point of view.

Written work

1. Write down the orders you imagine Pizarro might have been given before his departure for Peru.

2. In Act 1, scene 5 Pizarro challenges Estete to write to the King about him if he has a complaint. Taking into account the tension at the time, what might Estete report? Pull together all the information and make a summary, then decide what should be included in a brief report to the King.

3   A modern-day group of explorers visits Peru and finds evidence of the
    1533 massacre and related events. Their discovery includes rough
    drawings that might be described as a modern-day storyboard. Recreate
    this and decide what other evidence they might have found.

4   Using the information in the play as well as your own ideas, write a
    description of the crossing of the Andes by the Spanish army. This could
    be done as if you are one of the soldiers taking part in the crossing.

5   You are in charge of publicity within a company which is about to stage
    The Royal Hunt of the Sun.

    * Write a press release giving details of the exciting forthcoming
      production.

    * Design publicity material to highlight issues within the play that
      might attract educational establishments.

    * Write a very short eye-catching piece of publicity that might appear
      on a hoarding outside the theatre.

    * Design a poster incorporating essential information about the play.

6   * You are responsible for designing the set for the play. Write a letter to
      the producer of the play relating your anxieties over the prospect of
      creating a lavish set and costumes with a modest budget.

    * As the producer, reply to the letter. Outline ways in which the
      designer could create the set and costumes at a reasonable cost
      without compromising on quality.

7   *The play relies, almost entirely, on spectacular production, while the unwary
    assume it is an expression of something of deep significance.*

                                                        Plays in Review, 1965

    Write an essay saying to what extent you agree with this statement.

8   A number of critics felt that since the Pizarro of history was a brutish,
    unintelligent mercenary and Atahuallpa, as far as is known, a traitor and

usurper, Shaffer has falsified his materials. What arguments can you put forward to suggest that it is not a dramatist's responsibility to be historically accurate? Present your arguments in essay form.

⑨ Shaffer suggests that he is interested by the conflict between *two different kinds of Right* (page vi).
What do you think are the two kinds of 'Right' in this play?

Suggestions for further reading

Other plays by Peter Shaffer

Five Finger Exercise (1958)
The Private Ear and *The Public Eye* (1962)
The Merry Roosters' Panto (1963)
Black Comedy (1965)
The White Liars (1968)
The Battle of Shrivings (1970)
Equus (1973)
Amadeus (1979)
Black Mischief (1983)
Yonadab (1985)
Lettice and Lovage (1987)

Other titles

History of the Conquest of Peru   by W H Prescott
The historical account that Shaffer used as his source material.

Peter Shaffer   by John Russell Taylor
A study of Shaffer's works and career.

Sleuth   by Anthony Shaffer
A play by Shaffer's brother, also a playwright.

Films

Although Shaffer stresses that he is essentially a writer for the theatre (see 'The writer on writing', page iv), several of his plays have, in fact, been filmed – most recently *Equus* and *Amadeus*. There is also a film version of *The Royal Hunt of the Sun*.

Wider reading assignments

Maybe too much significance is attached to the fact that Peter Shaffer is a twin. His brother Anthony Shaffer is also a writer. Jules Glen, a specialist in psychology of twinship has researched the influence of twinship on creativity and has written many articles on Anthony and Peter Shaffer's plays. He has observed in his study of twins intense rivalry and attachment, a lifelong identification with the other twin, the sense of being an incomplete person, the desire for revenge and the wish to make things even.

These elements he observes are present in the conflict between the characters in Shaffer plays, between Andrew and Milo in Anthony Shaffer's *Sleuth*, between Pizarro and Atahuallpa in *The Royal Hunt of the Sun*, between Alan Strang and Dr Dysart in *Equus* and between Salieri and Mozart in *Amadeus*.

1. Compare and contrast the intense relationship between pairs of characters evident in some plays by Peter Shaffer.

2. *Peter Shaffer's plays are repeated variations of the theme of man's struggle for meaning in a world in which death dominates and religion holds no salvation.* What evidence is there to support this statement?

3. Compare the playscript of any one of Peter Shaffer's plays with its filmed version. What, in your opinion, is gained and/or lost by the transfer from theatre to large screen?

Longman Group Limited,
Longman House, Burnt Mill, Harlow,
Essex CM20 2JE, England
and Associated Companies throughout the world.

This educational edition © Longman Group Limited 1991
This edition first published in association with Hamish Hamilton 1991

First published 1991
Sixth impression 1995

Editorial Material set in 10/12 point Helvetica Light Condensed
Produced by Longman Singapore Publishers (Pte) Ltd,
Printed in Singapore

ISBN 0 582 06014 1

Acknowledgements

Cover photograph from the Ancient Art and Architecture Collection.

Consultants: Linda Cookson
Geoff Barton

The publisher's policy is to use paper manufactured from sustainable forests.

Longman Literature
Series editor: Roy Blatchford

Novels

Jane Austen   *Pride and Prejudice*   0 582 07720 6
Charlotte Brontë   *Jane Eyre*   0 582 07719 2
Emily Brontë   *Wuthering Heights*   0 582 07782 6
Charles Dickens   *Great Expectations*   0 582 07783 4
            A Christmas Carol   0 582 23664 9
George Eliot   *Silas Marner*   0 582 23662 2
F Scott Fitzgerald   *The Great Gatsby*   0 582 06023 0
            Tender is the Night   0 582 09716 9
Nadine Gordimer   *July's People*   0 582 06011 7
Graham Greene   *The Captain and the Enemy*   0 582 06024 9
Thomas Hardy   *Far from the Madding Crowd*   0 582 07788 5
            Tess of the D'Urbervilles   0 582 09715 0
            The Mayor of Casterbridge   0 582 22586 8
Aldous Huxley   *Brave New World*   0 582 06016 8
Robin Jenkins   *The Cone-Gatherers*   0 582 06017 6
Doris Lessing   *The Fifth Child*   0 582 06021 4
Joan Lindsay   *Picnic at Hanging Rock*   0 582 08174 2
Bernard Mac Laverty   *Lamb*   0 582 06557 7
Brian Moore   *Lies of Silence*   0 582 08170 X
George Orwell   *Animal Farm*   0 582 06010 9
            Nineteen Eighty-Four   0 582 06018 4
Alan Paton   *Cry, The Beloved Country*   0 582 07787 7
Paul Scott   *Staying On*   0 582 07718 4
Virginia Woolfe   *To the Lighthouse*   0 582 09714 2

Short Stories

Jeffrey Archer   *A Twist in the Tale*   0 582 06022 2
Susan Hill   *A Bit of Singing and Dancing*   0 582 09711 8
Bernard Mac Laverty   *The Bernard Mac Laverty Collection*   0 582 08172 6

Poetry

Five Modern Poets   edited by Barbara Bleiman   0 582 09713 4
Poems From Other Centuries   edited by Adrian Tissier   0 582 22595 X